W9-AEI-938

Saint Columban

Saint
Columban

FRANCIS MACMANUS

SHEED AND WARD – NEW YORK

© *Sheed & Ward, Inc., 1962*

Library of Congress Catalog Card Number 62-9108

NIHIL OBSTAT:
Rt. Rev. Msgr. James T. Clarke
Censor deputatus
October 20, 1961
IMPRIMATUR:
✠ Jerome D. Hannan
Bishop of Scranton
October 28, 1961

Manufactured in the United States of America

Foreword

THIS book is the result of a desire to see and understand a man who died more than thirteen centuries ago. It is an attempt to put together in a significant pattern the fragments of what was once a continuous reality. The reality was a man of unbelievably intense energy and devotion. His name was Columbanus or Columban or simply Columba, and he was a saint. The fact that he was a saint does not make the effort to understand him any easier.

Simplicity is always rather difficult except for rare people like poets, unspoilt children, some philosophers and, of course, saints. That simplicity called sanctity, that integration through grace of the human personality, always presents the biographer with more problems than he can master. How does one communicate sanctity, or describe it? The old hagiographers solved the central problem in their fashion. They collected and described miracles. Sometimes they borrowed miracles from other saints. Occasionally, when the humanity of their subjects intimidated them, they looked the other way, said nothing and passed on. Their intention was just as much to edify and to create living saints as to celebrate dead ones. It was not an ignoble intention. It was the intention of Columban's first and best biographer.

Columban moved through his age as the most ascetical of monks, as a founder of monasteries, as a castigator of tough, wilful rulers, as a missionary in a corrupt, half-christened civilization, and above all, as one of the begetters of the penitential spirituality which characterized Europe of the Middle Ages. It was more than just incidental that he came from Ireland into Gaul. In his epoch, he could not have come from any other place and been the kind of man he was.

This essay in vision really began more than a quarter of a century ago on the northern bank of the Loire a few miles below the drowsy river town of Beaugency. It was a July afternoon, and in the breathless heat, rooks drawled in the high trees that shaded the river path. Out under the sunlight the bleached grass was almost as white as the fine sand on the islands and bars in the diminished river. In the shade there was coolness enough for long easy sleep after a meal of bread and wine—good Vouvray—and a piece of cheese. I woke from a heavy dreamless sleep to the sound of voices.

Half-blinded by the light reflected from the drifts of white sand, I looked far out across the dry channels towards the current that groped its way between osiers and willows, and saw a long flat boat which two men were pushing and guiding downstream with poles. There was a mast for a sail. In the stern, five or six men were sitting quietly, their bodies swaying a little with every impulse of the boat. Then, just for an instant, my mind was filled with a most vivid illusion: I saw men in rough habits of untreated wool sitting with the meekness of prisoners in a long boat slipping downstream towards Nantes and the Atlantic: Columban and his monks going by royal command into banishment.

They were being banished from the monasteries he had founded and from the wilderness they had cleared, tilled and made to flourish through years of labour in the Vosges. Not for the last time, Columban had fallen foul of civil authority. On this occasion the authority was in the persons of a young passionate king and an old strong-minded queen of a Merovingian kingdom. He was also in trouble with some of the bishops of Gaul, who would be glad to see the last of him. It is not often in history that saints manage to bring themselves into disfavour with both Church and State at the same time.

Such a man as Columban was either conquers or is conquered. It was under duress and between armed guards that Columban and his monks had been marched for weeks across a kingdom and been pushed aboard a boat that slipped down the Loire to find at Nantes a ship which would rid Gaul of their pestilential presence for ever. Their destination was intended to be their own country, Ireland, from which they had exiled themselves in the name of Christ. But, as the reader will discover, kings had a habit of failing to coerce Columban, and this journey into banishment would, like other passages of his life, end most dramatically.

So on that July day on the bank of the Loire, something I had read and brooded over and then forgotten had been stirred up from the riverine depths of memory by the move-

ment of a boat, the sound of voices and the dazzle of summer light on the waters. I am quite sure I had not then read
the life of Columban which was written less than three
decades after his death by Jonas of Susa. What Jonas wrote
is the beginning and almost the end of all that one may
know substantially about Columban as distinct from
what Columban wrote himself.

As books go, it is a small thing, but very powerful and
full of a good man's awe before a saint. It excites the desire to see; and while Jonas does give many elements of the
picture that had been familiar to his contemporaries, he
stimulates rather than satisfies. Till after the Day of Judgment, his silences and reticences will tantalize readers.
Only for him, however, Columban would not be so well
remembered. In fact he might be an even more disputed
figure among the scholars. How easily does time hide away
even the giants!

One day as I wandered the narrow streets of Susa, I came
into the place where the centuries are annihilated by a
thing of stone. There stands the triumphal arch that was
erected by a Celtic chief and dedicated to the Emperor
Augustus. The chief of the tribes in the Cottian Alps was
in no doubt that he commemorated Roman greatness when
he had that arch raised and the friezes cut. As I stared idly
I remembered Jonas, born in this town, reared by a very
affectionate but stout-hearted mother and schooled here.
And for the moment, grotesquely perhaps, the arch seemed
to have no other purpose than to signify that here in Susa
in the early seventh century this obscure man had looked
on the arch all during his boyhood before he went south-

ward to Bobbio in the Apennines and was received in the
name of God by the abbot of a monastery who had himself
been received and blessed by the founder, Columban the
Irishman from the remote western island at the edge of the
known world.

Contents

Saint Columban

CHAPTER 1

The Island of Monks

FROM the western Irish headlands, men could look out only on the endless ocean where the sun was daily engulfed and watch the clouds that the tempering winds herded eastwards season after season across the island. The clouds brought the abundant rains, and the rains were life. Although they periodically flooded river and lake, waterlogged the rolling midland plains and soaked into the brown desolation of the boglands, they were the mother of the thick succulent grasses on which the cattle grazed and grew fat nearly the whole year round. Really harsh weather was brief in duration. Then the wild geese honked in the grey sky and cold caught the wings of birds. It was, as many writers were to repeat, a land flowing with milk and honey, genial in air and fruitful soil. *Melle fluit pulchris et lacte Scottia campis,* an Irishman was to write who became bishop of Fiesole where in the bleaching sun he may have gratefully recalled the cool curtains of rain drawing and wavering across his native landscape.

It was cattlemen's country. Cattle were wealth, units of currency, the penal fines put on transgressions, the price of slaves, and the spoils of raids and battles. But it was also woodmen's country. Forests were everywhere, oak and ash, elm and yew, beech and hazel, thickening the springy damp floor with the fall of centuries of leaves, pattering ceaselessly with rain drops in the long wet seasons, feeding domestic swine, squirrels, foxes, wolves, and the red deer and wild pigs that men hunted with hounds and spears. Deep among the trees there was refuge for hunted or rejected folk, for the outlawed, the crazed, the cattle thieves and those punished by banishment, for whom there was no secure place in the closely ordered farming communities that inhabited the hillsides, the valleys and the plains. There was also seclusion for those men who withdrew from all human companionship to pray in solitude. Poets were yet to come, in a few generations, who would praise that woodland solitude, loud with birds, as if it were the gateway of paradise.

The human companionship from which they withdrew was not that of villages, towns or cities. Of those, there was none. It was the closer companionship of kindred reckoned to many degrees of consanguinity, of parents, grandparents, children and grandchildren, cousins, nephews, nieces, as well as foster-children and concubines, all living in the circumscribed intimacy of the isolated farmsteads. The larger farmsteads that harboured the great family groups were like islands on the landscape. Behind the high earthen or stone embankments that rose out of deep exterior fosses, the houses sheltered down from the winds, cattle-raiders, thieves and prowling wild animals. Grass and briars knotted and bound the packed earth against weathering, and the earthworks looked like an upheaval of the green grassland and cleared woodland. Inside the guardian ring, the houses stood grouped, timbered, wattled, daubed with clay, and roofed with thatched reeds or layers of turf. They oozed wood smoke when, at mealtimes and in the colder seasons, the wind blew the wrong way. On the clay floors food debris and rubbish accumulated, the rejected fragments and bones that, nearly fifteen centuries later, would be treasure for patiently scrabbling archaeologists. Within the enclosure the animals were housed too when night fell, the herds of swine, the flocks of sheep and goats, cattle and horses. Each farmstead was a self-contained world in which a man could be born, could grow up, beget children and die, drive the beasts to pasture, guard them, attend to the lambing and calving, eat the same milk foods in summer and the salted meats of winter, and shelter beside the fire for the winter nights to tell or hear told stories about warriors, kings, battles and cattle-raids, and the other world. It was a slow seasonal life, and what seemed most permanent in it as the generations came and went was that high grassy rampart of earth or stone that walled the little world like a fort.

To the infrequent traders from Roman Gaul or to the even more infrequent merchants who had seen, say, the glittering city on the Bosporus where the Emperor Justinian ruled, the households in these ring-forts must have seemed exotic, as primal and organic and as far from the Roman conception of social life as the bees that hummed in the straw hives on the sward in the sunshine. Indeed, the houses were sometimes shaped like the hives. Inside the houses, as travellers might discover if they tarried long enough, life followed an immemorial organized pattern; and they might further discover that households were related by blood to households in comparatively small terri-

tories, and that these territories, the *tuatha,* were units of
more or less self-contained government, ruled by a *ri* or
king. The emphasis of life was on kinship and personal
rule, and within that kinship, that familial association, the
pattern was hierarchical and the grades of people were un-
equal. The aristocrats were the warriors and those whose
family descent could be traced to gentle forebears by the
genealogists. Between them and the workers in the fields
and the herdsmen, the servants and the bondswomen, com-
moners all, there were those who by skill in the crafts and
the disciplines had won a privileged status; and among
them were the poets and historians who celebrated the
rulers and kept intact the communal memory, the lawyers
who defined rights and duties, the metal workers, the medicine men and the musicians. For them ancestral tradition
was a thing created by the long succession of generations,
to be respected and venerated.

In hardly more than a hundred years, between the middle of the fifth and sixth centuries, the deepest of changes
had taken place in this society. Christian missionaries had
come from Gaul and Britain, and a pagan world was being
rapidly transformed not so much in external details as in
the inmost life of the people. A comparatively short while
after the death of Patrick—himself a herdsman working in
slavery for a pagan ring-fort household in his youth—exterior signs of the innermost change which he had initiated
as a missionary began to manifest themselves all over the
island. To these new Christians, and especially to their
children and their children's children, an image of a more
intensely desirable Christian life presented itself. They accepted it with astonishing single-mindedness and adapted

it to their way of living with creative energy. It was the image of the monk who by an uncompromising ascetic discipline detaches himself from love of father and mother, wife and children, from love of self and even of life, and abides in the monastic family. Knowledge of such a life and of its possibilities must have come through St. Patrick himself and later from Britain, Gaul and by devious ways from the deserts of Egypt. So widespread and fructive was this knowledge that one can compare it aptly to the rain falling like an abundant prolonged grace until even the rocky western headlands and the islands nearest to the setting sun became monastic sites.

Grace perfects nature. Grace fell; the nature was already there in social forms, receptive, closely-knit and worthy. With its emphasis on kinship and personal rule, on affective familial association and a hierarchy of social grades, the Irish pastoral order readily accepted the concept of the monastic family, bound by spiritual relationships in charity, ruled by the *abb* who was a sacred personage like the *ri*, subsisting by work in the fields, and guarding the enclosure for the sake of precious isolation. The independence of the ring-fort became the independence of the monastery; and those monasteries that shared a common founder were linked together in a kinship of the spirit as the households in a *tuath* were linked by blood. The respect for the *aes dána* became christened in the monastic respect for letters and learning in the native, as well as in the Latin and even Greek languages, for crafts in wood metal, and for the essential study of the Scriptures and the writings of the Fathers of the Church—an intellectuality that distinguished the Irish monks from those of Egypt and Syria.

The monks thought of themselves as spiritual warriors, fighters against pagan beliefs, errors, heresies, and especially against the rebellious, sinful and evasive self. In the phrase of Clement of Alexandria, they were "the elect among the elect."

The change to monasticism was rapid and profound. Armagh, the primatial see founded by St. Patrick, became monastic in its organization; and the ecclesiastical organization which he and his disciples had set up in the island became by the sixth century like a hollowed-out apple in which the bees had established a home. Before Columban was born the Church in Ireland was a church of monks. Many of the monks were hiving off from the warm, protective life of the native enclosures and going into mortifying voluntary exile as founders themselves and as missionaries in Britain, the Hebrides, the Orkneys, Shetland, and to the Continent. When Columban was still a young man, hardly more than a novice, in 563 St. Colmcille was in Iona.

2

About a hundred years before Jonas of Susa sat down to write what he had been so long preparing, a woman in Leinster who was heavy with child dreamt in the dead of night that a glittering sun rose from her breast and lit the world with a great light. So also had the mother of St. Ciarán of Saigher seen a star drop into her mouth. It was the storyteller's way of ushering a saint into the world with signs and wonders. It pleased Jonas. There was little else he had to tell about the birth and family of Columban.

From the few facts he provides, conjecture must take over to weave a tenuous web of suggestions. It is probable that Columban was the son of a highborn Christian household. He was noble in his bearing and handsome. He studied at home in his boyhood, probably learned his letters in the Psalter as other Irish saints like Brendan and Colmcille are said to have done, and wrote Latin as his first written language. Jonas says he studied from boyhood to manhood in grammar, rhetoric, geometry and in the Sacred Scriptures, the curriculum of Irish Christian schools which savours more of Romanized Europe than of native Celtic Ireland and suggests the presence of a learned tutor.

It has been conjectured that the territory in which he was born and reared lay between the rivers Slaney and Barrow; and that later when he went to his first school, he travelled north to an island in Lough Erne which was in territory that had been settled by kindred of the family to which he belonged. But before he made that journey to study under Sinell, who was most likely the abbot of the monastery of Cluain Inis in Loch Erne, he endured, according to Jonas, two kinds of personal trial, both by way of womankind.

Because he was handsome and attractive, he was besieged by the attentions of young women about whose motives Jonas has no doubt at all. He resisted. Jonas has him fighting with the round brazen shield of the gospel in his left hand, the *clipeus evangelicus,* and the two-handed broadsword in his right. Was this account of Columban's youth a genuine memory or a hagiographer's conventional device? If it was genuine, who could have told Jonas about so remote an episode? We may guess it was Gall. At any rate, the young Columban, troubled in his adolescence and anxious that he should not be distracted from his studies, went for advice to a woman hermit who lived nearby in a cell, probably a wattled hut far enough from any ring-fort to provide solitude. Jonas produces a speech she is supposed to have made, but reading it, we are reminded by its formality that it was one of his amiable weaknesses as a biographer to attempt classic flights of style. The hermit was no sybil. Her message was blunt and clear. She told the young Columban that fifteen years previously she had forsaken her father's house to fight temptation and sin. Since then she had never wavered under the grace of God, and if she were not a mere weak woman, she would have crossed the seas to find a more secluded retreat. "But you," she went on, "burning with the flames of youth, stay at home! Willy-nilly, you will find yourself in your weakness listening to the tempting voices. Do you think you can go freely in the company of women? Do you not remember that Adam fell through the blandishments of Eve, that Samson was seduced by Dalila, that David fell from grace through the loveliness of Bethsabea, that the most wise Solomon was deceived by love of woman? Away with you, young man, away from the ruin that has destroyed so many; turn from the road that leads to the gates of Hell."

It is clear that Jonas was representing in the manner of his time an important crisis in the young man's life. Frightened, Columban returned to his home. What happened there was as violent in emotion as the crucial fear that impelled him. It was the second personal trial, and it concerned his filial relationship with his mother. He told her he was leaving home. She pleaded with him, clung to the door so that he could not pass, wept, and threw himself across the threshold. She refused to give permission. He stepped across her prostrate body, asked her not to grieve, and set off knowing that he would never see her again. It was a sudden and hurtful act of detachment, the beginning of the long mortification which was to be his life. In her anguish, there is a most poignant expression of the feeling for kindred that had created, and was preserved by, the small worlds of the ring-forts. The whole event was a dramatic gloss on the words of St. Jerome: "The enemy holds the sword over me to strike me down; so what should I care for a mother's tears? .... The proof of filial affection in this matter is to be cruel."

In his account of the two ordeals, Jonas gives us our first clear view of the character of Columban, or at least, of one aspect of that character. We may wish to know more about the studious young man who renounced what he knew of the world on the advice of a woman hermit, but the wish is vain. Anything more that can be written about his boyhood must be unsatisfactory conjecture. Columban as a person disappears almost completely into the new monastic life, into the silence and isolation in which men were unmade and remade, frequently to emerge as spiritual giants who preached, worked wonders and miracles, travelled into exile as missionaries and founded monasteries of their own.

He left his native Leinster and, travelling northwards, put himself under the care of "a venerable man" named Sinell. Of Sinell nothing is known except that he established a community on Cluain Inis on Loch Erne and that he was a disciple of one of the most influential founders of Irish monasticism, Finnian of Clonard in Meath. Finnian was one of the great founders through whom, by his own personal influence and continual communication, contacts were made with monasteries in Britain, a liturgy introduced and a more detached knowledge of monastic organization. Under the influence of Gildas and of Cadoc "the Wise" of Llangarvan, he transformed his foundation at Clonard. Following the British example, he laid stress on study as part of the round of duties. He was abbot, bishop, and a renowned teacher who came to be called "Master of the saints of Ireland." He died when Columban was a child, but out of his monastery had come, among countless others, twelve saints and founders who were anciently styled "the twelve apostles of Ireland," and among them was Sinell of Cluain Inis.

In all the host of names, his was not forgotten when nearly a century later Jonas wrote about the island world of which he had had no experience, no history and no more than hearsay knowledge. Jonas wrote that Sinell was "famous for his holiness and for his learning in sacred things." The pupil, Columban, had not forgotten his first monastic master! Under Sinell, he was inspired with a love of the sacred sciences and taught how to think clearly and with intellectual curiosity and freedom. A memory of that freedom to seek for the truth by questions would return to him in his old age when he would find himself involved in a debate of great moment, and the memory would be accompanied by legitimate pride. The foundations of his learning were laid in Cluain Inis. While yet a young man, he had made sufficient progress to write a work on the Psalms (the language of his daily converse with God), as well as some other works including hymns and books of in-

struction. It is possible that at this time he wrote the verses
sometimes entitled *De Mundi Transitu,* which is taken
from the opening line. Some of the thoughts and even
phrases the verses contain appear in later writings, in a
sermon and a letter; and there may be a reference to the
ordeals that had been a fire in his blood. There are a few
quotations from the Bible as well as echoes of Ovid and
Ausonius. The theme is that this world will pass away; that
the beauty of men withers in old age; and that the radiance
of Christ's Face is to be more desired than the brittle flower
of the flesh—*flos carnis fragilis.* A few lines run:

> *Caveto, filiole,*
> *Feminarum species*
> *Per quas mors ingreditur,*
> *Non parva pernicies.*

> Beware, my little son,
> the forms of women,
> through whom death enters,
> no light destruction.

So Walker translates the lines which have the conciseness
and the dry wisdom of the Gaelic verse the Irish monks
themselves were to write in later generations when the
suspicion of heathenism had been lifted from the native
learning and language.

How long Columban remained in Cluain Inis we do not
know, but Jonas tells us that when he decided to become a
monk he set out for the monastery of Bangor, to place himself under the rule of Comghall, the most notable father

of monks in Ireland, well known for his insistence on study and strict discipline. Five or six lines of what Jonas wrote encompass a period of many years; and for all he has to tell of that period, Columban might as well have vanished from the face of the earth; which, in a sense, he did. He prayed, fasted, denied and mortified himself, taking up his cross to follow Christ. It is a description that could have fitted any good and fervent monk, unremarked and unremarkable in a family of faithful brethren. All that one can attempt to see, and then only dimly, is the monastery of Bangor flanked by wooded hills above a sandy fretted seacoast, and Comghall the abbot.

3

The monastery of Bangor was only a few years old, and Comghall had founded it. What he raised was one of the great and solidly founded monastic institutions that endured for centuries as the home of thousands of monks, the school of scholars, liturgists, scribes, missionary priests, and saints. He seems to have lived for some time on an island in Loch Erne, where his discipline was renowned for its intense austerity. It is probable that earlier still he had been a farmer and a warrior who had fought in wars, but the rigours of either occupation cannot have been as trying on body and spirit as his discipleship under a man who might justly be called the father of extreme Irish asceticism. And what this man gave to Comghall, Comghall gave to Columban.

He was Fintan of Cluain Eidnech, now Cloneenagh in

the barony of Maryborough West. He would have been at home in the utterly barren and hot sands of the Egyptian desert, subsisting on a daily handful of herbs and a mouthful of water and living under the flimsiest screen of Nile reeds. But he was living in a fertile pastoral land and neither the milk nor the honey would reach his lips. In a land of herds, there was not a single cow that his community could call its own. Neither milk nor butter was used or allowed. If milk were brought inside the precincts of the monastery, it was to be spilled and even the vessel that contained it to be broken. Food consisted of wild herbs and the drink was water. It was written in his praise: *Fintan fial, niro tomail re ré riam, acht arán eorna foeda is usci creda criad:* during his time Fintan never consumed but bread of withered barley and clayey water from the clay. In the Irish eulogy there is the hardness of bone hardly covered by the starved flesh, and the gritty taste of the earth.

Only exceptional monks could live by such a regimen. The impulse to maintain it must have been nourished by total dedication and an unceasing routine of prayer. We cannot tell how much Comghall took from Fintan, how he adapted or modified the fearful discipline so that men even a little less than exceptional might be able to live by it and not break their own spirits. What Comghall and Bangor lived by was harsh enough, but the monks blessed Comghall's rule and rejoiced in the family, the household, the *munther,* to which they belonged. In the famous Antiphonary of Bangor some monk praised the Rule and the household in a song:

Benchuir bona regula,	Good the rule of Bangor,
Recta atque divina,	Correct and divine,
Stricta, sancta, sedula,	Strict, holy, constant,
Summa, justa ac mira.	Exalted, just and admirable.
Munther Benchuir beata,	Blessed the family of Bangor,
Fide fundata certa,	Founded on certain faith,
Spe salutis ornata,	Graced with hope of salvation,
Caritate perfecta.	Perfect in charity.

It was not at all curious that the secular usage of the Irish word for household or family or kindred, that is, *muintir,* should have derived from *monasterium* as though the brotherhood of monks had become the model for the brotherhood of men. Saints established the relationship, and Comghall was among them. In his Rule, or at least in the Rule that is attributed to him, he ordained: "Love Christ, hate wealth, piety in you towards the King of the Sun, and smoothness towards men. . . . Let no one go from you to beg. Remain at home in prayer. Ever endure your poverty. . . . Love not a man's wealth. Thou shalt not sell; thou shalt not buy. . . . Beg not of a king in Ireland. . . ." From those words, "Love Christ," all the rest flowed: the detachment from wealth, the smoothness towards men (Columban sometimes forgot it), the abstinence from commerce, the subjection of religious to worldly power, and residence in the monastery to pray. If the monks could sing the praises of the *bona regula* that crucified the self in them, it was precisely because it crucified them. By continual prayer, fasting, work and study, the four forms which their activities took, they were remade in the image of the Cru-

cified One. One form of activity ministered to the other,
and all to the ultimate aim. The monks worked, fasted, endured austerities, studied, and on occasion withdrew with
the abbot's permission into solitary places so that they
might mortify the disorders of the flesh, purify themselves
in heart and mind, and thus be capable of more intimate
converse with God. For many monks this converse meant
ecstasy on the mystical heights.

In the context of Irish society, physical work had a special significance. In that society only those who were unfree
or of lower grades laboured in the ring-forts and in field
and forest. But the monks worked. They felled and
trimmed the trees. Columban's own disciples would arouse
admiration for their skill and speed with axe and wedge.
The monks built the oratories of which many were needed
since they were small; they built the timber or stone huts
which were the cells, the refectory, the scriptorium in
which the books hung in leather satchels, the storehouses
and other out-offices, daubed with wattle and wickerwork,
limed the walls, thatched the high-pitched roofs that threw
off the rain, and set up the nearest thing to a city that the
people had ever seen. They dug, ploughed—Fintan for-
bade the use of draught animals!—sowed and reaped,
herded the flocks of cows, sheep, pigs and goats that wandered in a land not yet fenced, fished when there was need,
cooked, scrubbed, and served the passing wayfarers with
the good food and drink they would not taste themselves.
The labour was continual and harsh. It was said of Comghall that he made life so very hard for his disciples by his
excessive rigour that before his death he suffered from a
fearful complex of diseases which were regarded by not a

few as punishment. There must have been sheer unre-
mitting effort of will behind much of the exacting labour in
all weathers, in summer's heat or winter's cold when the
icicles glistened from the eaves. To sustain them, these
men ate only one meal a day of poor quality at about the
ninth hour, that is, about three o'clock in the afternoon. It
consisted of vegetables, herbs, peas and beans, flour mixed
with water, and bread. This diet was a contradiction of the
enormous gross feasting that was figured in the sagas and
tales of kings and warriors. It made little of that sign of the
wealthy household which was the capacious bronze or iron
cauldron hanging and bubbling over the hot wood embers.
Since most of the monks came from well-to-do houses where
such cauldrons were hanging, the signs of contradiction
were all the more significant of profound change.

What the monks studied under Comghall can be sur-
mised with some certainty. They were men of two intellectual cultures, one native and Irish, the other continental,
Christian and Latin; one oral, and the other mainly written. At first after the coming of the Christian missionaries,
there had been what Father John Ryan, S.J., calls "a gulf
of separation between the two cultures" precisely because
what was native, conservative and even resentful, had been
impregnated with pagan pieties. But the gulf was narrow-
ing.

Study of the Latin language meant familiarity with both
pagan and Christian writings. In his various works Columban would give many evidences of this familiarity and
quote or echo Virgil, Horace and Ovid, as well as Prudentius and Ausonius, to mention only a few. He wrote and
quoted with the almost voluptuous love of language that

was to be expected in a man who had been bred in the native tradition of the spoken word as the only means of transmission, not just between man and man, but between the long generations. Yet all this secular literary skill was only an adjunct to what was the chief intellectual occupation of the monks. This was the study of Sacred Scriptures. The many-coloured fabric of the Bible became part of the tissue of their minds. So it would be with Columban. Whether he expounded theology, fought against heresy, or meditated on the transient things of the world, scriptural quotations came easily to his pen. In the scriptoria the most common volumes to be transcribed with pen and ink on vellum—an act of ascesis—were books of the Old and of the New Testaments which, in later decades, were ornamented and illuminated with figures adapted from the old native pagan art-forms. But not just for pride of learning or display! Study like the other forms of activity was directed towards that converse with the Lord. The monks studied that they might pray with better understanding and live in wisdom. In fact, it might be said that they lived to pray— pray in solitude, in the communal chanting of the Divine Office, in the innumerable blessings in the name of the Blessed Trinity, and in the chief act of worship, the Mass.

The Hours gathered and bound them into a community of prayer. Wherever they were within the enclosure, in cell or scriptorium, workshop or kitchen, or wherever they were in the fields, they hastened into the oratory for the Divine Office when the bell was sounded. It can have been at best a thin, shrill and non-resonant sound beaten from the outside of a box-like structure of bronze or iron, but its message was obeyed. It was as the voice of the abbot to whom obedience without qualification was to be given in all things. It may have been here in Bangor that Columban learned his strictness in this obedience to the bell, for he never accepted failure to hear it as an excuse for tardiness, and only the cook and the porter were allowed any latitude.

The central act of worship was, of course, the Mass, which was celebrated on Sundays and feast-days, probably also during the fifty days after Lent, and on the death of a friend. Usually it was celebrated at an early hour. There was much diversity of rite. Whatever the diversity may have been, there is reason to believe that every act and word, vestment, cloth and vessel used in the celebration was interpreted through depth after depth of significance from intensive meditation on the Mystical Body of Christ and the meaning of the sacrifice. From a tractate on the Mass included with the famous Stowe Missal, which is at least two centuries later than Comghall's rule in Bangor, one may choose a few examples of this religious symbolization. The chalice on the altar was the Church, and the altar symbolized the persecution on which it had been established. (Were the chalices in Bangor of bronze, or even of iron as Columban's was, since Our Saviour had been nailed to the Cross with iron nails?) The water poured into the chalice in three drops symbolized the influx of people into the Church; and at each drop the congregation prayed, saying first, *Peto Te, Pater,* next, *Deprecor Te, Fili,* and lastly, *Obsecro Te, Spiritus Sancte.* The Host placed on the altar cloth was a figure of Christ's Body laid in the linen sheet of His Mother Mary's womb. The Consecration was the plenary revelation of the New Testament which had been prefigured by the previous partial unveilings of the chalice.

4

The forts that stood like islands to enclose and protect
the great familial households were ancient and immemorial
like the forests or the hills, but here in Bangor as in other
places under the monks, they were new things, transformed
and transformative. Kindred through descent from kings
whose lineage the genealogists would attempt to trace back
to Adam, had become kinship in Christ, the second Adam.
The secular pride and life-lust of the highborn which the
poets and historians could nourish and stimulate with
encomiastic poems and tales of unconquerable valour in
arms, raids, spoils, battles and slaughters were submitted by
these men, the monks, sons of high households, to all the
mortifications of a most inclusive obedience.

For nearly thirty years of his life, Columban is lost
among them, a monk among monks who moves on san-
dalled feet and wears the coarse woollen hooded *casula*. He
is unidentifiable. Jonas, who would become a monk in
distant Italy because of these years in Bangor, has no news
of him. We cannot see Columban; we can only guess at
his presence as he walks a path between the rows of huts,
lifts his hand to bless or bows his head to receive a blessing,
slips into his place in the oratory for the recitation of the
Hours, teaches a class of young novices, or strides off on
some distant errand to another monastery for the Abbot
Comghall and prays as he carries suspended on a cord
from his neck the chrismal which contains the Blessed
Sacrament, the Companion of the travelling monks. He has

been ordained priest. He has his appointed place in the household. He has books to study, books and treatises and verse to write, full of voices and the echoes of voices from Horace, Virgil, Ovid, Ausonius, Claudian, Prudentius, Lucretius, Fortunatus, Juvenal, and Sedulius, Christian speaking to him and for him with pagan poet; and even from the pagan poets, especially from the great ones, wisdom can be drawn like honey from the comb:

O nimium felix, parcus cui sufficit usus. . . .

O greatly blessed is he who can do with little: Virgil and Horace were echoed for the expression of a truth which he, Columban, was proving in nerve and sinew. In the same verses he wrote then or would write, there was a phrase Prudentius would have approved about avoiding the distraction of the flooding swarm of things, *circumflua copia rerum,* the besieging pressure of creatures from which a monk withdrew his desires by a long process of detachment and by the unrelenting routine of discipline. He could live out all his days in Bangor and never leave it just as men lived out their days in the ring-forts, knowing and loving every hut and fence, field, tree, sandy inlet and frothing coast. But is not such love, good in itself, yet another attachment which one may renounce? There were yet more ways in which one could mortify and sacrifice the self, and of these, the last and the most permanent and crucifying and most terrible was exile: departure from all one knew, from place, monks, relations: utter exile. Colmcille had gone into such an anguish of exile in the Hebrides, and it would be written of him: "Like the separation of soul and body is the parting from one's brethren and one's native land and the going forth to distant foreign lands in exile and perpetual pilgrimage." Now, Columban in Bangor began to wish for such a separation.

He remembered the command God had given to Abraham: "Go forth out of thy country, and from thy kindred, and out of thy father's house, and come into the land which I shall show thee." But not being his own man, he asked permission from Comghall who, at first, refused. It was not easy for the abbot to make a decision. Columban was a priest, and priests were comparatively few in the monasteries. Columban was scholarly and intellectually very able and had been, if a tradition is correct, in charge of the monastic school of studies. Moreover, he was likely to be the next abbot of Bangor. Comghall turned the problem over in his mind, and in the end, putting his own interests below those of his monks and of God, he not only gave his permission but offered to give Columban a group of companions and equip them for the journey.

Who were the companions? And for what land were they leaving their kindred and their father's house?

There were twelve companions, a number that had an obvious spiritual significance. They gathered their books into their satchels, the Mass book, the sacred vessels and relics; and into wallets they packed food, probably hard-baked oaten or wheaten bread. Each man took his long curve-headed staff, and each man, it is likely, had been freshly tonsured from ear to ear across the front of the head in the Irish way and presented with a new inner tunic as well as a new coarse woollen *casula*, odorous with natural oils. There was Gall, the best-remembered, who was more than likely a priest; and Dichuil, possibly his own uterine brother; and a second Columban who, dying of a fever in

exile, would be held back from death by the prayers of his
great namesake; and a youth, Domoal, who would act as the
leader's *minister;* and Cominius, Eunoc, Equonanus, Lua;
and probably a bishop named Aidus. We have not got the
names of all the twelve. Jonas tells little of the story of any
of them, and hardly anything about the journey, which was
both a portentous adventure and a form of martyrdom very
nearly like death. He tells us that Columban gathered his
companions together, went down to the sea, asked for God's
blessing, and embarked.

It was about the year of Our Lord, 590.

CHAPTER 2

Into Gaul

THE voyage, we are told, was short and easy, but whether Columban and his companions first landed in Britain or in Brittany is a matter of dispute among the scholars. In whichever place the pilgrims landed, they did not stay long, according to Jonas, but rested after the voyage, and at length decided to go into Gaul. Even that decision was not definitive. If they should find the people there unreceptive to their preaching, they would move on to some of the neighbouring peoples.

All Europe stretched before them in which to find a place to preach, pray, clear ground, build, dig, sow and reap, and grow as a community, cell by cell. In comparison with the minutely regulated, silent, brotherly and purposeful life in Bangor, it was a world which seemed chaotic, troubled and almost beyond understanding. On Gaul of the Franks, the dense dark forests lay full of game and wild animals, and haunted dangerously by fugitives from the wars, displaced peoples, serfs on the run from the great villa farms, and misfits and criminals from the decayed Roman cities where bishop or official in barbarian service tried to preserve some social order, municipal services, and peace. Along the Roman roads that had not yet disappeared under grass and weeds and coiling briars, the Frankish nobles rode with their retinues, men armed with spears and swords, axes and polished shields. Their horse-trappings glittered with metal, glass, enamel and jewels. When they moved, the road was theirs and all men made way, even the Gallo-Roman wealthy landowners who, in the seclusion of villa estates, tried to remember and to ape the old Roman ways.

In that year of Columban's arrival in Gaul, a devout and scholarly bishop who was also an historian laid down his pen at the end of a long work. He was surfeited with stories of the violence and malicious madness of the Merovingian kings. Sitting in his most ancient city near his cathedral where the afflicted crept to the tomb of St. Martin for healing, Gregory the bishop of Tours had long meditated on the bloody feuds, treacheries, bestial crimes and assassinations, lusts, adulteries, sacrileges, fratricides, perjuries, burnings and lootings of the descendants of the Clovis who had founded the Frankish kingdom in blood and murder, and in a superstitious bargain with the Lord Almighty. Of the grandsons of Clovis only one was alive in that year. He was Gunthram of Burgundy, wise enough to be called the Good King by Bishop Gregory, who had also known the worst. The worst had been that brother of Gunthram's, King Chilperic of Neustria, who had ruled his share of the divided Frankish inheritance from Soissons. Soberly, Gregory had described him as "the Herod and Nero of the times." Seven years previously, Chilperic had been murdered by an unknown assassin, and Gunthram, who was already taking care of another murdered brother's son as well as the kingless territory of Austrasia, next adopted Chilperic's son and assumed care of Neustria. What had been broken apart in the Merovingian inheritance by violence was put together by the old man's affection.

Of that third generation of the house of Clovis, a few of the legitimate sons and two of their innumerable women have most bearing on Columban's story. They were Sigibert, who, holding court at Metz, ruled the territory of Austrasia that stretched from the Meuse across the Rhine into parts of Germany and Switzerland; Chilperic, who ruled from Soissons the kingdom of Neustria that lay between the Loire and the Meuse; and Gunthram of Burgundy, which included districts south of the Loire as well as the Rhone valley.

Columban was in the heaven-haven of Bangor when Sigibert of Austrasia, the best of the three, chose the daughter of the king of the Spanish Visigoths as his wife. She and her sister were famed all over the western world for beauty. Her name was Brunhilde. She came to Sigibert with a large dowry. Her charm, intelligence and integrity impressed Gregory of Tours, and Fortunatus celebrated her beauty in an epithalamium. Sigibert loved her well all his married life, which was short. But she had a beautiful sister and he had a most Merovingian brother.

Chilperic had the immense physical courage and energy of his line. Yet, he seems to have inherited much that was of the worst in his forebears, not the least quality being his frequently irrational sense of proportion. He was capricious in tyranny, an inventor of tortures, a glutton at table, and a lecher whose passions would make him the victim of a woman's conspiracies. He possessed considerable intelligence, but not sufficient to prevent him from considering no man as clever as himself. He wrote limping verse, some hymns (for he had a strong streak of piety like most of the Merovingians), tried to increase by royal authority the number of letters in the alphabet and to decrease by his Arian theology the number of Persons in the Blessed Trinity. As a reward for their services, he elevated some of his followers, layfolk, to the episcopacy, which already could display some venal, hunting, bibulous prelates. It was his fate to be figured in stone as Apollo with a lyre on a portal of the Cathedral of Notre-Dame of Paris, which is comprehensive enough to hold gargoyles and devils as well as saints.

This Apollo also desired a wife as beautiful as his brother's, and what he desired he usually obtained. To marry Brunhilde's sister, Galswintha, he repudiated his wife Audovera, but by this time he was dominated through his passions by one of the most striking women of the time, Fredegund, his wife's maidservant, a figure creeping sinuously, like a cat, to the place of power at the king's side. Within a tragic year Galswintha was strangled in her bed, and Fredegund, whom Bishop Gregory called the enemy of God and man, was Chilperic's queen.

In the years of war that followed and brought ruin to towns, farmsteads and vineyards, Queen Brunhilde's desire for revenge played a part in decisions. She did not rest until she set her husband, Sigibert, moving with the Austrasian armies. For a time a Lombard invasion of Gaul halted the strife. Gunthram of Burgundy, who was bearing the brunt of this invasion, appealed for aid; and Chilperic, who had been hard-pressed, made a peace of sorts and gave as *were-*

geld for the murdered sister her enormous dowry and five
Aquitanian cities. Brunhilde accepted the blood-price, but
she still waited for revenge.

Four years later—probably when Columban was a newly
ordained priest in Bangor—the brothers were at war once
again, burning every open town between Tours and Lim-
oges and devastating the valley of the Meuse. Again, Chilperic was hard-pressed. He asked for peace, offering large
territories, but Brunhilde induced Sigibert to refuse. The
Austrasian armies advanced into the heart of Neustria.
Chilperic's son and heir was slain, and he himself abandoned his capital, Soissons, and fled, while most of his
counts rode to Paris to do homage to the victorious Sigibert.
The pursuit continued until Chilperic was driven beyond
the Schelde. At Vitry, near Arras, Sigibert was raised on a
shield in the old triumphal Frankish fashion and saluted as
king of all the Franks. It seemed that the end of the fratricidal war was near and that Queen Brunhilde's sister was
to be avenged. Then, two murderers hired by Queen Fredegund came to King Sigibert with a message and, as he listened, stabbed him to death with poisoned daggers.

Her violent act changed the course of the violent story.
The Austrasian army dispersed; the Neustrian counts now
flocked to Chilperic. Queen Brunhilde and the dead Sigibert's four-year-old son and heir were seized at Paris and
imprisoned by Chilperic's followers, but the child was
saved by a faithful adherent, lowered in a basket from the
prison window and carried off to Metz. He was to be saluted
as king by the Austrasian counts and dukes and by the high
officials of the palace, who thus initiated their control over

the monarchy. Queen Brunhilde was robbed of her treasures and thrown into prison at Rouen.

She was still young and still beautiful. In Rouen she caught the eye of Merovech, son of Chilperic by the cast-off wife, Audovera. In the reckoning of Gregory of Tours, doom lay on the young man. One day, as he wrote, he was invited to Merovech's dinner-table, where he was asked to read something good for the soul, and Gregory, opening what he called the Book of Solomon, read out the first verse he saw: "The eye which has been turned in hostility against a father, the crows will tear from its socket." Merovech was turning, it could be said, against his father, who had charged him to lead an army against the Austrasian territories along the Loire. Instead, in love with Queen Brunhilde, he freed her from prison and persuaded the bishop of Rouen to marry them in his cathedral. King Chilperic came riding to Rouen in a storm of anger. The newly married couple fled for sanctuary to the bishop. Oddly, Chilperic temporized, and more oddly still in a life of treachery, he took his son, Merovech, to Soissons when he yielded himself up and forced him to become a tonsured monk. Queen Brunhilde escaped, or was allowed to escape, to Austrasia, and presently Merovech slipped out of the monastery and followed her. Again, Queen Fredegund acted. He had almost reached the frontier and safety when her agents overtook him and murdered him. The way of succession was now clearer for her own sons by Chilperic.

For greater safety, Queen Brunhilde removed herself and her young son, Childebert, to Burgundy where they found something like a home. His childless uncle, King Gunthram, adopted him as his son and designated him heir.

Gunthram, Gregory's "good king," believed that his childless state was a punishment for his sins, and his sins were
Merovingian. All his sons had died in their prime. The
lonely, ageing man poured out his affection on the child,
Childebert, for whom the joint kingship of Burgundy and
Austrasia was destined. But not before more warfare, more
devastation! For a while, Chilperic's armies swept along in
victory to seize Tours and Poitiers and all the north of
Aquitaine, but a rebellion among the oppressed Bretons
drew him aside. Queen Fredegund worked her way towards the full power that she desired for her children. One
son of her husband's, Clovis by name, stood between them
and the throne, and when two of those children died of the
plague that ran through Gaul, she accused him of witch-
craft and had him killed. But she could not always conspire
with death at her pleasure. Two years later her own last
surviving child died. She went crazed with cruelty, accused
persons in the court of the black art, burnt them, broke
them, and sent to his death that bishop of Rouen who had
married Queen Brunhilde and Merovech.

For a little while there was peace, forced against Brunhilde's will, between young King Childebert and King
Chilperic. One day in 584, Chilperic returned from the
hunt to his manor house at Chelles, and as he dismounted
from his horse with his hand on the shoulder of a servant
for support, a man stabbed him under the arm with a
knife and then pierced his belly with a second stroke—
"whereupon he fell down and breathed out his foul soul."
The festering revulsion of the saintly, cultivated man that
Bishop Gregory was lies in the attachment of that word
"foul" to "soul." Yet, it was not the end of Chilperic's

brood. He left Queen Fredegund with a son, Clothair, four months old, who was to survive all of them, who would be the second of his name, and who in a most fateful time would meet, fear, and honour the monk from Bangor.

Of all the brothers, grandsons of the great Clovis, there was left only Gunthram, a fond and not ignoble old man who, coming to Paris where Fredegund had taken sanctuary, spared her life and recognized her infant, Clothair, as the rightful king of Neustria. For his part, he wanted peace, but she would yet again hire assassins to make attempts on Brunhilde and Childebert, and fail. Peace there would be among the Franks, but there would be wars against the Visigoths of Spain, and there would be war on behalf of the Emperor Maurice against the Lombards in Italy. In Italy, Childebert, now twenty, in this very year of Columban's arrival in Gaul would be forced by famine and disease to make peace before the walls of Verona with the Lombard king, Agilulf—a king whom Columban would meet and impress.

Gaul had indeed suffered, and men could see hardly more than the pestilence of evils. Certainly, Gregory of Tours hardly saw more than the wickedness of the kings and of their women, and the depravities of the bishops they nominated and controlled. But these, in their sins of perjuries, sacrilege, simony, gluttony, drunkenness, and scandalous worldliness, were not the whole of Christian Gaul. For Gaul was pervaded by a creative religious energy. Even the fratricidal kings and their women could manifest intense genuine piety, sudden as their wrath. They could take pride in their Christian belief, hate heresy, build churches and shrines, and endow monasteries and convents.

All about and beneath the violence and surviving the devastations of sword and fire, communities stood sound in open and walled towns where able saintly bishops spent their lives not only as good pastors but as leaders of municipal governments and as the chief help of the poor, the sick, the hunted and the broken. The vitality of faith in the common folk drove them in flocks to the churches, the shrines, and out on the pilgrim roads. The bells still rang serenely above the hurly-burly of the wars and above the sound of the Merovingian hunting horns fading away along the rides of the vast forests.

2

A murmuring silence as of the deepest forest seems to envelope those first years of Columban and his monks in Gaul. Whatever Jonas of Susa learned of the journey from the northern coast into the heart of the country, if indeed he ever learned very much, he did not choose to set it down. He writes briefly of Gaul as a land in which wars and negligent bishops had brought about almost the complete collapse of religion so that only belief without practice remained. In this spiritual desolation the voice of Columban echoes. He preaches the gospel. He is utterly poor. He and his men are humble, unassuming, gentle and considerate. Charity between them is so potent that they act as one. They are never idle. They check the slightest stir of anger, arrogance or envy. They never speak a harsh word. So greatly are patience, gentleness and love developed in them that one would think the Lord himself lives among them. They hold what they have in common, and if any man of them ever attempts to make something his own, he restores himself to fellowship by doing penance in solitude. So many are the graces abounding in the monk, Columban, that in whatever home he stays, he draws all souls *ad religionis cultum.*

It is a rather set picture from which the detail has faded. It provides no more than a glimpse of a figure preaching or entering a doorway to bless the inhabitants in the name of God. Jonas does not tell us what tongue the Irishmen spoke or if they used Latin and interpreters when preaching in Frankish or Gallo-Roman households. It has been conjectured by scholars that they may have used Latin-German vocabularies like the one in Irish script in a library of St. Gallen in Switzerland, which tradition attributes to St. Gall himself as author; and Gall was renowned for his ability to learn languages. This vocabulary contains a list of words relating to building and agriculture, travel by land or sea, the human body, the seasons and the weather, herbs and beasts.

However Columban communicated with the people, it was the fame his preaching brought him that determined the next episode of his career and inaugurated the succession of achievements for which he was most remarkable in the eyes of contemporaries. But before we can see him and his companions clearly as they drive into the primeval silence of the forests which are to be their home, we come upon a confusion in the records.

Jonas says that Columban's fame reached the court of King Sigibert. Sigibert was dead since 575. According to the chronology that some scholars have worked out for

Columban, his arrival in Gaul occurred about fifteen years
after that date. It seems that Jonas was in error and that
the king of Austrasia and Burgundy who heard about
Columban's fame was Gunthram.

At any rate, Gunthram was in need of whatever consolation a man like Columban could bring him. In his last days
fear shadowed him, and he never moved without a guard
of armed retainers. Too many of his house had died by
poison, dagger, in battle and pestilence. It was not so long
since he had ordered the slaughter, at his dying wife's request, of the doctors who had failed to heal her; nor was it
long since three men had died violently as a result of his
commands because the remains of a slain buffalo or auroch
had been discovered in the jealously preserved royal
hunting grounds in the Vosges.

Columban and his companions came invited to the
court and preached to King Gunthram and the courtiers.
They were well received. The king was so moved—was
there an upsurge of hope in him?—that he begged Columban to remain in the kingdom, and he offered him
whatever he should ask. Columban replied that he did not
wish to enrich himself by the work of others but only to
follow the example of the gospels in so far as the weakness
of the flesh would allow him. He quoted: "If any man
will come after Me, let him deny himself and take up his
cross and follow Me."

The king replied: "If you wish to take up the Cross of
Christ and follow Him, look for a more secluded place of
retreat, but do not leave our territory nor pass to neighbouring peoples, so that at the same time you will increase
your own reward and give us the chance of salvation."

It was an appeal that Columban could not refuse. He
began to search for "a more secluded place of retreat," and
soon he found it in a wild and deserted region of the
Vosges, among the trees and underbrush in an old tumbled-
down Roman fort. It was the *castrum* called Anagrates, in
the modern hamlet of Annegray in the department of the
Haute-Saône. What was left of it lay in a sort of no man's
land on the vaguely defined frontier between the kingdoms
of Austrasia and Burgundy. Long ago, Attila had passed
this way, burning and destroying, with his stocky, big-
headed horsemen, the Huns. To reach the retreat, Columban and his men had to plunge into the deceptively
silent forests, the free domain of wild beasts and fugitives,
and climb craggy wooded slopes up the valley of the
Breuchin river. On a mound that may have first been a
Celtic tumulus, they began to build the first of the
Columbanian monasteries on the Continent.

Jonas does not tell us how they built, though it is certain he had heard accounts of how Columban's men could
work. They repaired a ruined temple of Diana to make it
serve as an oratory and dedicated it to St. Martin of Tours.
They scavenged stones from the rubble, felled trees for
timber for the huts that were the cells and the refectory,
and cleared the ground. There was nothing grand in what
they raised, for they had brought with them as builders
the lowly rustic traditions of the ring-forts.

For food they had nothing except herbs, roots and the
bark of trees, the provender of wild herbivores. It was a
wretched diet for toiling men. It was no wonder that one
of them became ill of a fever. Jonas recounts the story of
the remedy they provided—and of their relief from the

remedy—as if it were the most matter-of-fact happening
in the world. For three days they prayed and fasted from
all food for the sake of the sick man! On the third day
when they were nearly spent with exhaustion, they suddenly saw in the doorway before them a man of the
neighbourhood who led pack-horses laden with bread and
vegetables. He explained that he had come because his
heart had told him to bring of his substance to those men
in this desert place who endured such need for Christ. He
handed over what he had brought and then asked them to
pray for his wife, who had been sick of a burning fever for
about a year without any hope of recovery. Columban
called his monks and together, starving and exhausted, they
prayed for the sick woman. Then Columban blessed the
man, who returned to his home to find his wife sitting
in the house in the whole of her health.

As edifying biographer, Jonas is in his element. He
passes from that story to yet another about hunger as
heroic as the hunger of the hermits in the legends of
Egypt. The monks continued to mortify themselves and do
penance. All desire for pleasure, *omnis voluptas*, died in
them, Jonas says, thus giving us an insight into their prolonged, harsh and unwavering domination of the self. For
a period of nine days it happened that they were again
without proper food except herbs and bark, and again relief arrived unexpectedly. A hard day's march away over
that rough terrain, there stood the monastery of Saulcy,
and the abbot, probably a Breton, was named Carantoc.
In a dream he was instructed to send help to Columban
and his family in the wilderness. When Carantoc awoke
he called his cellarer, Marculf, told him about the vision,

and ordered him to bring whatever he could gather to help Columban in his need. Marculf loaded carts and set off, but when he came up into that wild country he could find no path. He let the horses go forward of their own accord, and—Jonas exclaims at the wonder of it!—they found their way to Columban's door at Annegray. For Marculf as for the biographer it was a miracle, and on his way homewards he told everyone he met about what had happened. He became, in fact, Columban's first propagandist, and he was effective. Crowds of people began to throng to Annegray, especially the sick, to ask for the medicine of prayer for their afflictions.

Here with these crowds came the perennial problem of the men who, in Egypt or Syria, Gaul or Ireland, had renounced wealth, lived for prayer and become renowned for holiness. The world they fled from pursued them. In their virtue they were the world's need, but the need of their virtue was solitude.

At Annegray, as at Bangor and many of the Irish monasteries, it was the practice of the monks who advanced in the process of prayer to withdraw completely on occasions from communal life and to live in utter solitude in caves, hollows in hillsides and the depths of the woods. Among the solitaries fasting became more intense and prayer more ardent. They practised prostrations and the heavy agony of the cross-vigil, in which the monk prayed with outstretched arms as though he were nailed to an invisible cross. It was a life that had its spiritual as well as its mental and physical dangers, and only those most advanced in the way of prayer and monastic discipline were allowed it, and then not for long. The reward for the soul could be something like the gliding flight of a bird above the top-most mountain peaks: wordless colloquy with God. Irish poets of a few centuries later would put into the mouths of hermit saints lyrical words to express this desire of the finite for familiarity with the eternal: *Crist mac Dé dom thaithigid* . . . I should love to have Christ, Son of God, visiting me, my Creator, my King, and that my mind should resort to Him in the Kingdom in which He dwells.

Columban searched for a hermitage and found it on one of his long solitary explorations of the wilderness. These withdrawals of his, characteristic of his life, satisfied deep emotional and intellectual, as well as spiritual, needs. He was a man of very strong emotions: he could love with a racking intensity, and also hate. His temper was volcanic. Even the best of the monks, relying on him as their father in God, calling on him for counsel at every hour of the day to his, the only solitary hut, inquiring for directions about this and that in all the manifold labour of building, felling trees, digging and sowing, even the best of the monks could become trying in this continuous communal association. It was, of course, an abbot's burden. Again, he needed long undisturbed spells for meditation and for working out the details of the Rule which he was to write down.

One day he walked through a very dense part of the woods, reading in a book of the Sacred Scriptures and meditating. A question entered his mind: whether it would be better to choose injury at the hands of men or the savagery of beasts. It was more than an academic problem. The reality of the forests inhabited by wild animals as well as wandering savage men could press it home. Frequently making the sign of the Cross and praying, he decided that

he would prefer the savagery of the beasts because it
involved no sin, while the rage of men could involve the
loss of souls. In a little while, one part of his problem was
put to the test when, roused from meditation, he saw
twelve wolves approach and stand around him. He remained absolutely still, saying, *Deus, in adjutorium meum
intende; Domine, ad adjuvandum me festina.* The wolves
draw nearer and touch the skirt of his clothes. He yet
remains calm. Then the wolves turn from him and wander
off among the trees. They smelt no fear from him. He continued his walk, and soon the second term of his problem
presented itself. He heard the voices of many men among
the trees. They were members of a band of the Suevi who
lived in the forest and practised brigandage. The voices
receded and he was alone once more. The point of the
story as Jonas writes it seems to be that Father Columban
preferred wolves.

Another day, he walked even deeper into the forest,
climbed up among the conifers above the site of the
monastery, and discovered the hermitage that would serve
his need. It was a hollow scooped out of a huge rock, and
brambles overgrew the opening. Breaking his way in, he
entered a bear's den, and the bear was at home. He told
the bear to leave, never to return, says Jonas, and the bear
departed to find another den farther from Annegray.
This shelter, some four hundred feet above the valley of
the Breuchin, was to be Columban's *carcair.* From here he
could look down and see below among the trees the huts
and oratory of the community, enclosed in the repaired
vallum of the old Roman fort.

Here he used to retire alone on the eve of Sundays and

of saints' feast-days so that he could pray without interruption. The food he ate was what he found at hand, herbs and berries and the little wild apples called *bullugas* by the people; and his drink was water. As servant to run on errands between the monastery and the cave, he sometimes brought young Domoal with him. It was Domoal who also carried water up the hill from a spring. On one occasion after Columban had been in the cave for many days, Domoal began to complain under his breath about the hardship of not having a spring near at hand.

"Son," said Columban, "make a hollow in the rock. Remember that the Lord drew water from the rock for the people of Israel."

As Domoal approached obediently to strike the rock, Columban prayed. The water flowed in a perpetual spring which, as Jonas wrote more that fifty years after the event, *usque in hodiernum diem manet.* And what flowed in the days of Jonas yet flows, as the people above that valley can tell when they show the cave to visitors and point down to the site of the monastery. In that fountain destined to flow for century after century because a tired boy was pitied by a saint, Columban or indeed any of his people would have delightedly perceived a symbol and drawn from it some sharp parable about the spiritual things that endure and refresh the soul in the arid transience of the world. The parable might be said to have more ironic truth than they even guessed. The strong lines of the Jura remain against the sky, but the dense forests have disappeared, the wilderness that the monks cleared and tilled, and all the monastery itself which they almost died of starvation to erect. Perhaps it would be no surprise for

them to see—as a visitor would see more than thirteen
centuries later—the mortal destiny of Annegray: a plain
wooden cross; part of an old wall on a farmstead, and in
a yard beside a spring of water, portion of an early Christian sarcophagus serving as a trough to hold potatoes!

This destiny might make the founder grieve. He must
have loved that countryside, possibly with an affectionate
attachment which to his ascetic mind could become dangerous as any earthly love. When the number of monks at
Annegray increased, he did not look far for another and
more suitable site for a larger monastery. He came upon
it eight miles from Annegray and lower down the valley
of the Breuchin, that river which took its name from a
Celtic goddess of waters, Brixia. This had been all Celtic
country. Here, Julius Caesar had wintered his troops and
met the Sequani, and all across the land Rome had laid the
marks of her civilization in the military forts and stations,
roads, towns with temples, villas, schools, baths and guardian walls. Where Rome had been, the barbarians had come
as invaders, leaving the deserted places that Frankish nobles
hunted for deer, buffalo and wild boar.

The monks fished the Breuchin. It was a good river for
fish, although Gall, who is remembered for his skill with
net and line, did not always agree with Father Columban
about where they might have good fortune. Indeed, Columban told Gall one day to fish the Breuchin, but Gall
went his own way to the river called the Ognon, cast in
his net and saw a shoal of fish turning back as though from
a wall. All day he cast and caught nothing, for it seemed
that the fish were in league with Father Columban in the
matter of obedience. Gall told the story himself many

decades later to the wondering biographer, Jonas. In the
evening he returned to tell the abbot of a wasted day, and
he was upbraided for not having gone where he was told.
"Go back at once," said Columban, "to the place I spoke
about." Gall went quickly, cast the nets and caught so many
fish that they could hardly be held.

Perhaps it was in Gall's company that Columban wandered down the valley of the Breuchin to the place on
which he would build the second and most famous of his
foundations. What he came to was wilder and more awe-
inspiring than any primeval wilderness. Beside the Breuchin was a chaos of toppled masonry. For nearly a century
and a half, the living green things had moved in to establish dominion, trees bursting through pavements and
walls, bursting arches and columns apart, villas, temples,
towers and city gates. Men had once lived and thrived
within the gates of Roman peace and security. Under the
smothering briars and brambles, the statues of Roman
officials lay with the statues of the gods, broken-nosed and
mutilated. In places the mildly mineral and therapeutic
waters that had supplied the thermal baths oozed out into
stagnant, scummy pools where, once the air grew chill,
vapours fumed and wreathed visibly. The birds had it all
now with the wild oxen, the wolves and the bears. This
ruination had been brought afar from the steppes beyond
the confines of the Roman world, and if Jonas knew how
Attila and his Huns had ridden in fury down this valley,
to this place Lixovium (later written as Luxovium),
scaled the walls, taken and burnt the town, he did not
bother to tell. It was enough for him that here Columban
found the site for the famous monastery of Luxeuil.

It was about the year 594. Gunthram was dead. The young Childebert, under the constant surveillance of Queen Burnhilde who was regent in the eyes of Pope Gregory, ruled over the kingdoms of both Burgundy and Austrasia, which included this tiny patch of chaos that the monk Columban now wanted. Who else could desire the rubbled lair of wild beasts and the desolation? Through the good offices of a courtier, Chagneric, one of whose sons would be schooled by Columban's monks with the sons of other Burgundian nobles, the abbot was given the ruins.

The monks set to work, hacking away the undergrowth, felling the trees, and building with the stones the Huns had toppled. Restored walls became the monastery enclosure, that symbol and reality of separation from the world. The monks built cells, a refectory, a school, and a church that was dedicated to St. Peter, and consecrated by Aidus. They were not left without help. Novices arrived. More and more children were sent for schooling. More and more penitents travelled into the wilderness for the private confession of sins and the spiritual consolation that the monks provided.

Not one, but two communities were growing up and thriving round the figure of Father Columban. Presently there was to be a third, Fontaines, three miles to the south of Luxeuil where the marshes were drained and reclaimed and good crops planted so that the land became the granary of the monasteries. Time passes quickly in the monastic life. Suddenly, it seems as one reads and meditates on the words of Jonas, Columban is the centre of the most intense activity—building, felling trees, burning out stumps, shaping timbers, sowing, reaping, teaching, instructing, receiv-

ing novices and scholars for the schools, visiting penitents
and Frankish nobles with their families, wayfaring priests,
the pious and the merely curious. He travels on foot the
eight miles back to poor primitive Annegray and the
cave on the hillside, or the three miles to Fontaines.
There are sixty monks and over two hundred disciples,
among them Chagnoald, son of Chagneric the courtier,
Donatus, son of the duke of Upper Bungundy, and his
cousin, Waldelenus, son of another duke—names to be
remembered. To all of them, Columban is father as
well as the *anam-chara,* the "soul-friend" without whom, as
the Irish saying had it, a man is like a body without a
head. Although he had men of proven worth and virtue to
act as *praepositus* during his absence, there must certainly
have been times when he was in peril of becoming lost in a
tangle of exigent details—that *circumflua copia rerum*—as
in the thorny undergrowth of the forest. The familial spirit
of Bangor, the knowledge and experience of discipline and
of the whole way of life that one carried, as it were, in one's
bones, were not now enough to infuse the great growing
group of communities with what Columban considered to
be the true monastic soul. Among the increasing numbers
of monks and disciples, the Irish were now comparatively
few. They all must know by what it was they had come to
live together. It was time to write down the Rule in
which, as Jonas would say, the discriminating reader or
listener will discern the holy man's mastery of the spiritual
life. He might have added that one may also discern the
holy man himself.

CHAPTER 3

The Rule

FOR more than thirty-five years Columban had lived in monasteries. He had absorbed monastic discipline until it was his nature. As father and leader, he had journeyed with a group of monks through a strange country where despite change of location, the rigours of travel, near-famine, and the perils and desolation of forests and cities, he had maintained community life intact. Jonas would tell how men wondered at the closeness of the community bonds on these men in whose minds the image of the soldier was seminal. Like a crack platoon trained to rebuild rather than to destroy, they had moved into the ruined places where Roman soldiers had once maintained the conquering Roman routine of garrison and camp, and they had dominated the wilderness with axe, spade, adze and plough, and humanized it by their handiwork.

Columban, then, knew monks as he knew himself. Alone in his cave above Annegray, or alone with quill, ink and parchment in his cell in Luxeuil, or even walking the woodland and river paths he and his monks had beaten out between the triad of settlements, he could meditate on the perfection of the monk, using as inspiration and mould of thought familiar words from the Scriptures, from the writings and sayings of the holy men of Cluain Inis, Clonard and Bangor, the fathers in the desert, Cassian, and St. Jerome. Let a monk live in a monastery under the rule of one father and in the company of many monks: and from one he may learn lowliness, and from another, patience; from one, reticence, and from another, gentleness. Let him not do what he pleases or wants. Let him eat what he is bidden to eat, complete his share of the work, and submit himself to whom he does not like. Let him come weary to his bed, walking almost in his sleep, and let him rise from sleep before it is finished. When he suffers injury, let him keep his silence. Let him fear the overseer, the *praepositus* of his community, as a master, love him as a father, believe that whatever he commands is for his good, and let him not pass judgment on the judgment of a senior.

All of these precepts and many others like them were concerned with social perfection in the monastic order, but preceding and infusing them as the essential principle which Columban expressed in venerable words, almost the first he wrote down: First of all things, we are taught to love God with the whole heart and the whole mind and all our strength, and our neighbour as ourselves.

The Latin in which he wrote his monastic constitution has been called crabbed and irregular in style—a note-jotter's Latin, perhaps written down not all at once but as occasions presented themselves. Certainly not all of the regulations in the documents that have come down to us in many and various manuscripts belong to what he himself wrote. His successors added, subtracted and interpolated, but such changes should not be a cause of surprise, because the spirit he bequeathed by example and word was vital and creative of monastic life, and where life is, as he knew, there is change. In his way he was often poignantly conscious of change, of flux, of transience, and in one of his sermons he said finely: *Quod enim sum non fui, et non ero, et unaquaqua hora aliud sum, et numquam sto:* For what I am I was not and shall not be, and every hour I am different and never stay.

Although the words of the Rule reflect, impersonally, the intensity, the vigour, the passion and the authority of his personality, there lies over them after the centuries an appearance of utter anonymity, like the features of a stone saint or king on the frost-pocked and wind-blasted figured shaft of a Celtic cross. But looking at the stone in the right low, oblique light and meditating on it and always remembering that here is an image of one who lived and breathed, one begins to discern vaguely the character of the living being—and of his brethren. This Rule, one discovers with excitement, is about and for ordinary men, the old, the young, veteran monks and mere boys, who wish to be unmade in the image of fallen Adam and remade in the image of Christ, and who will unmake and remake themselves in humility and charity through absolute obedience; through a silence that will account every spoken word by its effectiveness in making good men better and in keeping peace; through a sparing use of food—vegetables, beans, a porridge of flour mixed with water, and a small piece of bread, to be taken once a day in the afternoon; through such a disdain of property as will leave them "satisfied with the small possessions of utter need," since cupidity is a leprosy for monks; through a complete suppression of self-esteem and vanity; through a chastity that goes to the depths of the spirit; and through a routine of communal and private prayer that divides out the hours of darkness and daylight.

This moral code which concerns the interior disposition of the soul belongs to the first, the *Regula Monachorum,* of the two parts which he wrote. Except for the section that deals in seasonal and mathematical detail with the Divine Office, it consists of general principles, and it is more of a treatise on the monastic life than a monastic constitution. In military terms, it is a statement of objectives and an expression of an *esprit de corps,* not a handbook of drill, tactics and strategy. As such it attracted and inspired monks of later centuries. No other writings of Columban's have been preserved in so many ancient manuscripts. St. Benedict of Aniane, first reformer of the Benedictines, would quote repeatedly from the *Regula* in his *Concordia Regularum,* but his passion for uniformity would be rather foreign to what Columban had conceived. Here, in Columban's words, were first principles. Perfection was to consist in the rigorous and wholehearted execution of a comparatively few fundamental precepts under complete loyalty to the *abb,* the father. Details of the communal life such as other monastic founders formulated and codified minutely were to be left to the custom of the monastery—except in the regulations concerning the performance of the Divine Office.

These regulations came out of a habit bred into the daily activity of his body and the movement of his mind. In them he showed how in custom he carried Bangor with him and how in experience that was like instinct he carried with him also the northern procession of the seasons, the long winter and the shorter summer nights. In an old St. Gallen manuscript it would be written of him—the truth of it would bring enormous anguish upon him—that he was a most unyielding follower of Irish traditions—*traditionum Scotticarum tenacissimus consectator*. Yet in the traditions of the Divine Office which he followed and brought to Annegray, Luxeuil and Fontaines, he looked to both the weakness of men and the varying march of the stars across the night skies.

He knew that the performance of the office of psalms and prayers in the canonical manner had been variously bequeathed by different authorities. There was no rigid uniformity. Quoting Cassian, he would also recall the Egyptians who kept to the same canonical number of twelve psalms, both on short summer nights as on long winter ones, so that what seemed small to some monks during the long darkness became burdensome and heavy enough during the short summer darkness and caused exhaustion rather than healthy fatigue. His system would not be uniform. The three Hour-offices of the day, at the third, sixth and ninth hours, would remain the same all the year round. For each of them the monks would interrupt work to assemble in the church and recite three psalms "together with an addition of versicles." These versicles or intercessions were for, first, the monks' own sins, then for all Christians, next for priests and the other orders consecrated to God, then for almsgivers, after that for peace among kings, and lastly for the monks' enemies that God should not account as sin persecution and slander by them since "they know not what they do." At the two night-offices, at nightfall and midnight, twelve psalms at each were to be chanted, but towards morning the variations would follow the seasons, the number of psalms increasing from June the 24th with the lengthening of darkness until November the 1st. From that date—Samhain, the Irish winter, the time of locked doors and the long storytellings in the ring-forts—the number of psalms at Matins would be thirty-six until February the 1st—the spring—when the decrease began.

Since Saturday and Sunday were special days, the Matins were special. By the time the winter cursus arrived, seventy-five psalms were being sung at each day's Matins, *ita ut totum psalterii inter duas supradictas noctes numerum cantent,* so that within the two aforesaid nights they sang the whole psalter, the Irish "Three Fifties."

In nothing were the monks so bound in community as in this regulated chanting of the Divine Office. Six times a day when the bell was rung they came together in the church, and they came promptly, leaving work in field or forest, within the enclosure in cell, garden or kitchen, or rising in the darkness from that broken sleep of theirs. Under penalty, they washed before entering the church. Only the cook and the porter were allowed to be tardy in their coming, since a bubbling pot can defy even a Father Columban, while neglect of a visitor at the gate could mean a failure in charity. Every sentence of psalm or of intercession, all the blessings and genuflections and prostrations, united them in spiritual intent and in physical movement. Under penalty, they were precise in their chanting of the psalms, knowing that even a cough would be a defect, or a smile, or especially loud laughter unless, of course, "it has happened pardonably." In that little qualification, like a gentle afterthought, there is a most charming touch of sophistication. All the brethren together at the ending of every psalm should uniformly bend the knee in prayer if bodily infirmity does not prevent it, and say three times in silence: *Deus, in adjutorium meum intende, Domine, ad adjuvandum me festina.*

2

Visitors to Luxeuil became more and more numerous. Whether they arrived for a night's shelter or to be shriven of their sins and spiritually consoled, they must have shared the impression which is common among visitors to enclosed monastic communities, that is, of having entered a world new, very strange, and completely different to their own. They were welcomed at the gate by the porter in the name of the Blessed Trinity, fed in the guest house, received and blessed by Father Columban or his *praepositus,* given a bed and perhaps allowed to watch that quiet-paced movement of robed and cowled men towards the dimly lit church and to listen to the carefully uttered psalms and prayers that were the monks' most sustained form of speech throughout the whole day. It was order, activity and reticence foreign to the mode and aim of their lives, whether they were Frankish nobles or Gallo-Roman landowners, court officials or merchants, such as might anxiously keep their minds on the varying and frequently ruinous quarrels of the Merovingian kings.

In the fields and woods beyond the enclosure, there arose

the sighs and noises of the night, the wolves padding down a forest path, a bird flapping its wings in the heart of a tree, a beetle droning, an owl hooting, leaves lifting and fluttering as the wind changed after the death of the sun; and farther away still, a villa or a long low thatched farmhouse deep in sleep where watchdogs cocked their heads to howl at some late traveller clattering by on a weedy Roman road; and farther away still, a town walled round where the king slept and his men guarded the gates, seeing first the enemy in all who came. But here in Annegray or Luxeuil or Fontaines, there appeared to be a prefection of brotherhood and order in chant, genuflection, movement, work and all human association. If visitors sometimes felt envious and longed for such peace for themselves, they could know that other men had shared that feeling and that longing.

Columban had been a monk for too many years not to know that in every individual as in the entire community there were innumerable possibilities for thoughts, emotions, words and deeds that could destroy this most desirable concord. The very closeness and continuity of association could drive an unwary monk into himself and exacerbate individuality and crankiness. Eccentricity could chafe and gnaw at the bonds of association until they were frayed tenuously. There were native defects in manners, deportment and character that might well teach patience and fortitude to some monks but raise bad temper in others. There were monks who talked too much or too loudly, who contradicted vehemently and indulged in recriminations, told silly tales, poured out excuses, left the church door open, forgot prayer before work or a meal, frequented cells without permission, prowled around the kitchen, cut the refectory table with their knives, messed the table with flour or beer or water, spoke while eating, scattered crumbs, blamed the porter for not being punctual in his duties, or came to the altar unkempt or unwashed or in the night-habit in which they had been sleeping.

These peccadillos and faults could be catalogued with their appropriate censures and punishments as school-masters of another time might catalogue the predictable round of schoolboys' misdemeanours. This is more or less what Columban did in the *Regula Coenobialis*, the Communal Rule, which is the necessary complement of the *Regula Monachorum*. This penal code, which prescribes penalties for infringements of the Rule and breaches of Christian refinement, appears to have been composed in a more desultory manner than the inspirational document. Not all of what has come down to us was Columban's own work, but even the first nine chapters or sections which some scholars attribute to him are of so severe and harsh a mind that they, along with the later additions, were claimed unjustly by one scholar to have been a Benedictine fiction, concocted to discredit Columban! While admitting to the severity, one may be doubtful of the harshness. The quality of harshness is relative. The same night frost that drove Frankish noble or easy-living Gallic bishop to the blazing fire and gourmandizing on suckling pig and veni-son, fish and game, sweetmeats and deep draughts of strong beer and hot spiced wine, became for the monks, slipping from hard bed to church, a tonic stimulant of drowsy senses. In Columban's eyes, what he asked and got from his monks did not seem exorbitant.

He praised and encouraged moderation, for he saw the universe and man's energies and inclinations in a dialectic pattern. Men must keep themselves from all excess by a splendid temperance and a true discretion—*per temperantiam gloriosam et veram discretionem.* This true Discretion was to be the product of a purified sense of reality, of a discernment refined by grace, prayer, mortification, discipline, detachment, work and study. In a sermon delivered late in his life, when in fact he was living in northern Italy and had only a few years to run, he spoke about this purified sense by which a man should look on what shall be rather than on what is. "For what is not, shall be," he said, "and he should think on what he does not see through those things which he does see." Thus, the whole world becomes like a forest of sign-posts pointing towards eternity. "No other outward thing ought to be loved, according to the reckoning of truth, except eternity and the Eternal Will . . . The wise man should love nothing here since nothing lasts. . . ." But in achieving this condition of detachment and attachment, one had to walk the world with true Discretion.

In his concept of true Discretion, there is a tension which he, who was fond of elaborate images, might well have compared to the delicate poise of one of the tight-rope walkers that he might have seen in some travelling show on one of his journeys across Gaul. One sentence of many about Discretion in the *Regula Monachorum* refers to this consciousness of balance: "While we must always keep ourselves from one side or the other, according to the saying" —he quotes Deuteronomy—" 'Never swerving to right or left,' we must hold our course straight onwards, that is, by

God's light . . . ." This balancing was manifest in his literary style, especially when he was drawing on his intimate
and affectionate knowledge of the Latin classical writers.
Both the principle and the style are evident in his listing
of penalties in his famous *Penitential,* in which he uses an
axiom of ancient medical theory to remedy spiritual op-
posites—*Contraria contrariis sanantur.* More striking examples of the effect of the principle on his thought and
style may be found in his sermons, or in that loving letter
which he wrote to Domoal, the boy who struck water from
the rock. "Be helpful in humility," Columban wrote, "and
humble in authority, simple in faith, cultivated in habits,
exacting in your own concerns, unconcerned in those of
others, . . . hard in the easy things, easy in the hard, diverse
in smooth circumstances, smooth in diverse ones, . . .
friendly to the honest, rough to the dishonest, gentle to
the weak, firm to the stubborn . . . respectful to the
worthy, merciful to the poor . . . forever fearing for the
end but advancing in certainty."

In justice to the *Regula Coenobialis,* which prompted
so many critics to charge him with fearful harshness, it is
right to keep in mind his principle and desire of moderation. Many of the faults listed in this Communal Rule arose
in the dark side of human nature where the physical can
overrun and confound the spiritual, and where words,
admonitions and good counsel can so often fail. "Will a
man by talk alone," he would ask, "cleanse his house of
dirt, or remove the dusty heaps of filthy rubble by speech
alone?" Like the places themselves, Annegray and Luxeuil,
men who would become good monks were primitively
disfigured by the dust and rubble of an aboriginal invasion

and catastrophe. They needed heroic human and super-human efforts for restoration.

Thus, according to his Communal Rule, there was to be that ascetical exercise of frequent confession before the single meal of the day and before bedtime. There was also, of course, the Sacrament of Penance. Men like Finnian of Clonard had stressed the power of penance to atone for every sin. "Confession and penance liberate from death," wrote Columban. Not even the smallest sins were to be omitted. This is the essence of the Communal Rule, and all else that follows—the listed faults and penalties—is no more than a penal code jotted down without an exacting regard for order.

It is in the penalties that critics appear to have discovered cause for the accusations of monstrous harshness. One might reply on his behalf with his own words from a sermon. "What kind of training is it," he asks, "that is without the sorrow of chastisement?" He goes on to say that there is grief as well as toil in the learning of any craft. There are blows for the musician's pupils, and fatigues and sorrows for the doctor's students. "But if, then, such and so many pains are borne untiringly for temporal and unsure rewards, what ought we to endure for eternal, true and sure ones . . . ?" What, indeed! Many of the penalties which Columban prescribed consisted of blows inflicted, it is probable, with a leather strap on the hand.

The monk who did not say grace at table and who failed to respond with an Amen, was to be corrected with six blows. There were six blows for the monk who spoke without need while eating; six for him who spoke with a shout, and six for him who did not bless the spoon with which he

supped. This matter of blessing the spoons in the community would be recalled as something peculiar against Columban's memory a dozen years after his death when the
rebellious monk, Agrestius, would appear before the
Council of Mâcon. It says much for the general acceptance
of corporal penalties that Agrestius did not complain about
blows but rather about blessings. The occasions for earning
the one must have been nearly as abundant as the occasions
for performing the other. There were blows for monks
who forgot to have their lighted lamps blessed by seniors;
for monks who did not pray before or after work; for monks
in choir who coughed at the beginning of a psalm; for
those who took the blessed bread with unclean hands, that
is, the *eulogiae,* the bread or wafers distributed to all,
catechumens included, who were not prepared or able to
receive the Eucharist. For the brethren who told idle tales
to others without censuring themselves—an imposition of
silence or fifty blows. There were similar penalties for
monks who contradicted roughly or rudely, condemned
the porter for not keeping his hours well, told lies, and who
went behind the back of the overseer, the *oeconomus* or
master of household activities, and got the abbot to reverse
a decision unwittingly.

If these details of faults and corporal punishments are
expressions of the character of Columban, then one must
confess that it is not easy for layfolk to understand him with
sympathy; but it must be added that the modern world
which might fail to understand him because of this rationalized application of physical violence has not rid itself of
violence! It must also be added that the blows were not the
only penalties. There were penalties of imposed silence for

such faults as loud unrestrained speech. Indeed, imposed silence was frequently commuted for blows. Fasting, prayers, and the recitation of psalms were used to punish messy servers at table or for careless cooks. For monks who were obstinate and contumacious, there was a sort of ostracism, a banishment to the cells to do penance in private until their good will should be made known and through humility they could be joined again to the brotherhood. Their restoration depended on themselves. Indeed, one must never forget that they were free to leave the monasteries and the rigours of discipline.

The wonder is not that many did not leave but that so many men flocked to the three households and accepted of their own free will the iron rule of Father Columban.

3

Inside and outside the enclosures of Annegray, Luxeuil and Fontaines there were stories to be told and heard about Columban. Whatever Jonas of Susa may have neglected, avoided or assumed as being too well-known to be told again in his life of the founder, he did not neglect the stories. Like a good storyteller, he tells them with comparatively little comment or moralizing. The stories succeed one another rapidly. The details in them are few and clear but vivid, like broad scenes in simple stained glass against a good light. When he is able, he names his informants, his eyewitnesses, the living men to whom he had gone patiently for the bits and pieces of the larger story of the Irishman.

Almost all the stories about the three communities belong to the world outside the enclosures. They are happy stories, tender, warm with the harvest sun, or shaded by the deep forest where the wild beasts and the smaller animals emerge from the secret perpetual twilight to play God's game for a little while with one of God's special friends. The hardships of the long journeys that Jonas undertook while he was piously collecting material for his book must have been well-rewarded when, in refectory or cell or garden, he sat with some veteran monk who had known Columban, gathered and memorized these *fioretti;* and nodded in wonderment.

Much of what he heard was about Luxeuil. Once in harvest time when Columban had spent some days in the hermitage above Annegray in prayer and fasting, it was made known to him that many of the brethren were sick of various ailments and that there were hardly enough healthy men left to look after them. He went down to Luxeuil, examined the sick monks, and then ordered all of them to get up from their beds and help to thresh the harvest. Those in whom the fire of obedience burned high arose immediately and set about flailing the wheat on the threshing-floor with confidence. When Columban saw how abundant were faith and obedience in his sons, he called out, "Stop. You must rest after so much sickness and work." Those who had obeyed and instantly gone to work were astonished when they discovered that no trace of their sickness remained to trouble them. Father Columban ordered a meal to be prepared so that all might refresh themselves in joy, but he warned the disobedient (*accidia* is subtle and can take on many forms) that their illness would last longer, and so, to their wonderment and Jonas's, it did last.

Another day, Columban and the monks were reaping wheat on one of the monastery farms. It was, as the story-teller told Jonas, a day when a mild and gentle breeze was blowing from the south. One of the reapers was the storyteller himself, by name Theudegisilus, and he cut his finger so deeply with the sickle that only a small piece of skin held it to his hand. He just stood still while the blood dripped from his wound on the stubble. From the distance Columban—did he never relax his watch!—called out that he should continue and finish the work begun with his brethren. Theudegisilus told him what had happened, and then Father Columban rushed to him—there is always angelic speed in his tenderness—touched the finger with spittle, and immediately it was completely healed. Theu-degisilus could recall for Jonas the zest with which he bent again to the reaping, and he could show the very finger that had been wounded.

There was not always sun and gentle south winds for the harvest. One time at Fontaines, a new field produced a heavy crop, but the weather went against the reapers. Storms of wind and rain threatened to beat the grain out of the heads and lodge them. Full of faith, Father Colum-ban summoned his monks to cut the harvest. They walked out into the downpour of rain, surprised and silent, and as they handled their sickles, they watched the abbot. What they saw, and afterwards related until it came to the pen and parchment of Jonas, formed one of the strangest of the stories.

At the four corners of the harvest field, Columban placed four monks who were full of faith, three men from

Ireland named Eunocus, Comininus and Equorianus, and Gurganus, a Breton. Then he returned among the reapers and began to work among them. All round the field the rain fell, but none fell on the field itself. A hot sun burned down upon the reapers and a warm breeze blew. They reaped the whole field.

Something similar to what happened to Theudegisilus also occurred at Luxeuil to a priest of the neighbourhood. His name was Winioc and he was probably a Breton. Jonas almost certainly heard the story from Winioc's son, Bobolenus, who became a distinguished abbot of Bobbio, but he does not say whether Bobolenus was born before or after the father's ordination. Winioc appears to have been a blameless but a very inquisitive man who frequently visited Columban. One day he followed Columban up the mountains where monks were felling trees and trimming timber. He noticed in wonder how easily and skilfully the workers split the trunks of the oaks with wedges. It is likely that his curiosity brought him too close to the work. A wedge flew out and cut him to the bone in the centre of his forehead, so that the blood ran freely down his face. When Columban saw this, he fell on his knees in prayer, then rose and, touching the wound with spittle, healed it. Only a faint scar could be seen.

Another day, this same priest, Winioc, arrived at Luxeuil and followed Columban wherever he went. One gets the impression of a faithful, affectionate hound dogging the abbot's sandals. When they reached the barn where grain was stored, Winioc looked in and declared that there was not sufficient grain to provide bread for so large a community, and he began to reprove Columban for neglect.

"If," replied Columban, "God's people serve Him faithfully, they will never know hunger." He then quoted from
one of the psalms: "Never did I see the good man forsaken,
or his children begging their bread." To drive home the
point, he added: "He can very easily fill this barn Who fed
five thousand men with five loaves."

That night Winioc remained in the monastery. In the
morning he happened to be passing the barn, and through
the open door where the steward was standing, keys in
hand, he saw that the storage space was filled with grain.
He asked who had sent the corn or what train of waggons
had carried it.

"It's not as you think," the steward answered. "Now
look and tell me if you can see the tracks of waggons or
mules on the ground. These keys never left my possession
all night. But while the doors were locked, God's bounty
filled the barn."

Winioc scrutinized the ground thoroughly for tracks of
those who might have brought the corn. He found nothing.
Then, giving back psalm for psalm, he cried out: "God can
spread a table for his servants in the wilderness."

The wilderness and its creatures surround the monastery,
but for the monks, and especially for Columban, the
deserted places are sweet and populous solitudes. It was
to a high deserted place above the young waters of the
Moselle that Columban went one day with two of his
disciples, a boy named Sonicharius, who was still alive in
the days of Jonas, and a monk named Autiernus. This
monk wanted to go on a pilgrimage to Ireland, probably to
see the land, and especially Bangor out of which the Irishman had come. But Columban said: "Let us go into the

wilderness and find out whether it's God's will you should make this journey or remain with the brethren."

So they went up into the mountain country and took only bread with them. After twelve days only a few pieces were left, and the boy, the monk and the abbot must have been very hungry. In the evening about mealtime, Father Columban told his two companions to descend the valley and bring back whatever food they could find. They climbed down the valley of the Moselle and discovered a fish-trap which shepherds had set in the stream. Of the five big fish that were in the trap, three were alive, and these were carried back to the abbot.

"Why," he asked, "did you not take the five?"

"Two were dead," they replied, "and we left them."

"You will not eat these," said Columban, "until you bring the others as well."

They descended once more and hurried back with the other two fish, and then Father Columban, reproving them for not having accepted the manna they had found, told them to prepare a meal and eat.

In the eyes of Jonas and of Sonicharius, who lived to tell him the tale, there was something miraculous in the finding of food in the hour of need. The miraculous is the point of most of the stories, though a few of them could have been explained without calling on the direct intervention of the supernatural; that sickness, for instance, which laid low nearly all the monks in Luxeuil, who recovered when they roused themselves at the abbot's command to the sweat of purposeful work. The miraculous was the primary material of the hagiographers of those centuries, and they were not concerned so much with describing the human nature

which grace worked on as with chronicling the wonder-
works which they regarded as warranties of the grace. Almost despite them, the men emerge from the carefully
fashioned shrines.

Again, Columban is walking, as he loves to walk, in the
wilderness shut off from sight or call. Among the dense
thickets that grow near one of the farms, he comes upon
the carcase of a stag that the wolves have pulled down and
killed. A bear is lapping up the blood, having already eaten
part of the flesh. Columban draws near, forbids the bear
to damage the hide because it is needed for shoes, and the
bear at once obeys and ambles off. Columban returns to the
monastery and orders the monks to remove the hide. As
they enter the thicket, they notice a great flock of birds of
prey hovering all round and not venturing to descend on
the carcase. The odour of the dead meat draws down these
carrion birds in flight, but then, as if something deadly
were intervening, they swing away.

It is another miracle for Jonas, and as a miracle it is
remembered by the monks. Implicit in the story as in so
many others is the theme of the restoration of man's
dominion, disrupted by the Fall, over all creatures. This
theme runs through many Irish stories about holy men: a
fierce boar is tamed and becomes St. Ciarán's servant and
first disciple; St. Moling's fox eats a hen belonging to the
brethren and then steals another to replace it from a con-
vent of nuns, atoning for theft by rapine; a stag holds up
a psalter on his antlers for St. Cainneach; and St. Colman
keeps a cock, a mouse and a fly as his servants and grieves
for them when they die. In another story about Columban,
Jonas makes the theme more explicit by commenting that

through the great power of God which He gives to His servants, they are honoured not only by the homage of men but also by the obedience of the birds.

The bird in the story was a raven. One afternoon at mealtime in Luxeuil it flew down and carried off one of the gloves which Columban wore to work and had left outside the door of the refectory. The meal eaten and grace said, Columban came out, searched everywhere for the missing glove, and then said that the only creature that could have taken it without permission was the bird that had refused to return to Noe in the Ark. This was the reproof scriptural and majestical:

"I will not feed its young again," he said, "unless it brings back immediately what it has stolen."

While the brethren stood and watched, the bird flew down among them with the glove in its beak, waited as if for punishment, and made no move to fly away until Columban told it to be off.

Jonas had no doubt about the founder's power over creatures of earth and air. Frequently he had heard stories about this power from one of the most remarkable disciples of Luxeuil, Chagnoald, son of that Chagneric who had helped Columban to obtain the royal grant of the monastery lands. Chagnoald had been in Luxeuil since boyhood. It was as attendant or minister to the abbot in the wilderness that Chagnoald had witnessed his converse with the birds and beasts. He had seen them come at the call, rubbed down and patted until they frisked and gambolled like puppies around their master. He had often seen a squirrel running from the topmost branches of the trees to obey the summons and to sit on Columban's hand or shoulder.

It was Chagnoald, the grown man and bishop of Laon, who told Jonas about those wonders and testified to them.

They are testimony to a depth of tenderness that even so rigorously self-disciplined a man as Columban might well fear. He could lock up grief for someone dead—seventeen of the brethren were to lie in their graves in Luxeuil before he would be banished from the place—though sometimes he could not stop the tears from flowing and revealing the intensity of his love. He feared love because it could signify mortal attachment. During the period of banishment, he would write to comfort the brethren from whom he had been forcibly parted and to counsel one of the best of them, the same Attala who would become his immediate successor as abbot of Bobbio and friend and informant of Jonas. He would advise him to be many-sided and versatile in government of the brethren who obeyed with faith and love. "But," he would add, "you must fear even their very love, because it will be dangerous for you." There would be danger if they hated and danger if they loved. "You must know that both, either to love or to hate, are real; in hatred peace perishes, in love, integrity." He feared that the wholeness of the dedicated man would be flawed by too much human love.

As he wrote, did he recall with a pang of old but still living grief the days when one of his very dearly loved monks lay dying of a fever in Luxeuil? The monk's name was the same as his own, Columban, and he was one of the twelve of *Munther Benchuir* who had sailed with him from Ireland and journeyed across the breadth of Gaul. Common effort, hardships and adventures shared, daily association in thoughts, actions, ceremonies and prayers as well as the bonds of fostered charity could weave be-

tween these men such a fabric of affection as would hold
them together more strongly and variously and subtly than
they could ever know—until the day of death.

The younger Columban knew he was dying. He prayed
for a happy departure. When he was on the point of death
and confident of the heavenly reward which he had sought
through long slavery, he saw a man clothed in golden light
approaching him and heard him saying:

"I cannot yet lead you out of the body because the
prayers and tears of your father, Columban, prevent me."

Was it the delirious dream of a fever in which, released
from the acquired control of discipline, the younger Columban's love for the older acknowledged and reflected
the older man's love for the younger? Whatever it was, the
intense vividness of the dream shocked the sick man awake
and he called for the attendant, Theudegisilus, the same
monk whose finger had been healed in the harvest field.

"Hurry," he said, "and bring Father Columban to me."

Theudegisilus hurried and found Father Columban, almost a ghost himself from the years of fasting and labour,
and he was praying in the church and weeping. Immediately the abbot comes to the dying brother and asks what
he wants.

"Why do you keep me in this burdensome life with your
prayers? They are standing by to lead me away, but they
are prevented by your prayers and tears. Loose these bonds
so that the heavenly kingdom may receive me."

Columban, their common father, is struck by fear. He
beckons all to assemble. The dying man is given the Body
of Christ as viaticum and the last kiss of peace. Then the
chant for the dead is sung.

In the death of a son, something of the father dies too.

In filial death, Columban would die seventeen times. But the empty place in the choir, the empty seat at table and the empty bed, would be filled as new men were accepted. For the sons that died, sons were born. One man was, if we interpret Jonas correctly, accepted before he was conceived and born to his distinguished parents.

There was at that time, as Jonas tells—the time must have been after 596 or 597—a duke named Waldelenus who ruled the peoples between the Alps and the Juras. He had no children. He and his wife, Flavia, came from Besançon, Urbs Vesontionum, to beg for Columban's prayers so that they might have an heir to their wealth.

"If," Columban said, "you promise to dedicate to God the son He will send you and allow me to be his sponsor at Baptism, I will implore God to send you not only this son who is to be dedicated to Him, but others as well."

They promised to do as he asked and returned home. A son was born to them. Once more Duke Waldelenus and his wife travelled to Luxeuil, this time to show their son to Father Columban and to give thanks. Columban took the child in his arms, blessed him, and at his Baptism received him from the font, naming him Donatus, and then restored him to his mother. Years later the boy came to the monastery for schooling. He would be one of the many good men on whom the Rule would leave its profound marks. He would become bishop of Besançon and build in that city of his father's a monastery for men under Columban's Rule. The walls of the ancient fortification would serve as the walls of the monastery which would be called the Palatium. Like godfather, like godson!

4

All who came to Luxeuil did not come, however, to renounce the world and wear the habit and the Irish tonsure;
and all were not noblemen's sons. From the country far
about the three foundations where Columban and his
monks were already legendary for holiness, the people
flocked for "the medicaments of penance." They had, of
course, their own bishops who held the keys of discipline,
and their own priests. Yet, they travelled the forest and
mountain roads and tracks to seek forgiveness for their
sins beside these monks. Why they did this partly explains
why the monks were already a legend.

They did it for a very human and understandable reason.
Here in the monasteries they were, as sinners, hidden from
the world, and their repentance and punishment were
private. Their shame as sinners was kept between them
and God. In the world from which they flocked, the system
of public penance was still carefully maintained, and the
penitents were publicly, conspicuously and deliberately
marked off from their fellow Christians. Sickness or the
imminence of death or episcopal dispensation could secure
immunity, but in health they stood withdrawn in the
churches with downcast eyes, like mourners. This separation, symbolic of spiritual separation, was most terribly
and dramatically emphasized when, during the sacred
ceremonies, the time came for partaking of the Eucharist
or receiving special blessings forbidden to sinners. For
then, the ostracized ones cast themselves prostrate on the

church floor with wailing and lamentation and waited
there until they were raised up by the bishop, who prayed
for them and then dismissed them so that they might per-
form in private the assigned modes of penance for the duration of the appointed times. When these times reached
their end, the offences were absolved and once more the
sinners could return and be part of the congregation.

The system was severe. It must have called for resolution
to the point of heroism in many individuals. For the in-
ordinately self-respecting, the vain, the proud, the shy and
the retiring, it must have been an agony. But here among
these monks from Ireland, there was an escape into man-
suetude, a paternal feeling for human weakness, and a
merciful promptitude and secrecy. The monks did not and
could not exercise public censures. They were not diocesans, nor, according to the traditions of their native land,
subject to diocesans. In any case, public censure was not
of their way. Their way, something they had brought with
them from among the *ultimi habitatores mundi* with the
Rule, the tonsure, the absolute poverty and other customs,
was a positive, realist and therapeutic approach to sinners
and sins. It was their millennial and perhaps greatest gift
to Europe.

In Gaul it was summed up and roughly codified in what
is called Columban's *Penitential*. This document, like so
much else that time has left of Columban's work, is disputed among scholars in its authorship, in its parts, and
in its antiquity. According to some scholars it appears,
however, that he wrote two penitentials: one shorter, less
explicit and concerned with monks and ecclesiastics, which
he either brought with him from Ireland or wrote during

the early years in Gaul; and the other, more detailed in its treatment of individual needs, which he may have added to the first when penitents crowded to the monasteries. This second part is chiefly devoted to the laity.

It is a grim anatomy of their sins, but more than an anatomy. It also contains the penances to be performed so that the sentence of absolution may be effectual. Here are the perennial sins whether in thought or deed: murder, violence between brother and brother, infanticide, fornication, sodomy, bestiality, adultery, lust in the heart, robbery and theft, false witness, slander, perjury, and gluttony with food or drink. There were also the sins that were relics of the dying pagan beliefs that lurked in remote places in the depths of the forests and the recesses of the mountains: ritual feasting in pagan temples, worship of the old gods and of idols, and the practice of magic for the destruction of enemies or to excite carnal love. It was the old world of old Adam, but it was the new world of penance for the Frankish rulers and their peoples, and for the mixed populations on whom autochthonous Celtic traditions and imposed Roman civilization had laid their impressions.

The characteristic features of Canonical Penance are absent. There are no solemn public reconciliations with the bishop, no lifelong disabilities, and no obstacle to receiving absolution more than once. The Columbanian way is private and individual. It is punitive, but it is also medicinal, reformative as well as reparatory. There is not only pardon but the removal of evil effects, and the restoration of spiritual health.

The first words of the *Penitential* contain the essence of

it: "True penance consists in the avoidance of sins which one must repent of, as much as in weeping for sins committed." But since men in their weakness do not avoid sin, "the measures of penance must be known." A scheme of these measures has been handed down by the holy fathers. In this regard Columban's mind goes back to Ireland, to Finnian of Clonard, whose code was his chief source, to the Welshman Gildas, and to the Irish tradition of the *anam-chara*, the soul-friend, the repentant sinner's companion and advocate before God. At least fifteen of the canons in his *Penitential* can be traced back to Finnian, who also uses the principle that contraries may be cured by contraries, that is, the garrulous is to be punished by silence, the sleepy with vigils, and the deserter with expulsion. There was a diversity of penances to match the diversity of offences. And here Columban had in mind the image of the medical doctor who prescribes different medicines for different diseases. The *anam-chara*, the spiritual doctor, must know to a nicety how to treat all ailments, *ad integrum salutis statum debilia revocare*, so that the sick might be restored to full health. Accordingly, Columban sets down some prescriptions that derive from "the traditions of our elders," *juxta seniorum traditiones*, and from his own understanding of cases.

Among the canons for the laity, the first concerns murder. Whoever killed his neighbour had to do penance "as an unarmed exile for three years on bread and water." After three years he could return to his own people and pay the obligations of affection and duty to the relatives of the slain; and thus, having made satisfaction, he could be

restored at the discretion of the priest to communion with
the faithful.

The very terms of the penance: the unarmed exile when
to go unarmed meant loss of dignity and grave danger, the
separation from comforting familial custom, the fasting,
and the humane payment of the dues of affection and duty
to the relatives who had been deprived of them by the kill-
ing—these terms belong to an older European world, not
necessarily merely Celtic, though they were part of the Celtic concept of law. The same concept which Columban,
and Comghall his master, and Finnian, who had been in
turn Comghall's master, had seen at work in Irish society
in disputes about violent deeds was brought into play in
another canon. If any layman, the canon runs, sheds blood
in a brawl or wounds or disables his neighbour, let him be
compelled to restore all the damage he has done; or if he
cannot pay, let him look after his neighbour's work while
he is sick and call in a doctor; and after the recovery, let
him do penance on bread and water for forty days. In another canon, one concerning theft, restoration of a stolen
ox or horse or sheep is to be made, as well as penance on
bread and water; but for the habitual thief who cannot
make restitution, there is penance on bread and water for
a year and a hundred and twenty days, and he has to give
an undertaking not to repeat the offence; at Easter of the
second year, he may communicate on condition that out of
his own labour he gives alms to the poor and a feast to the
confessor who had adjudicated on his penance. Finnian of
Clonard mentions a similar feast.

The Franks understood these terms of punishment. The
terms are part of their world as their sins are which Gregory

of Tours noted wearily, the murders, gluttonies, robberies, fornications, and especially the perjuries. The penance for perjury was, in its way, more severe than any other in the *Penitential,* more severe even than the penance imposed on a cleric—that is, a man in minor orders—for murder. For murder, a cleric faced ten years on bread and water in exile from his native land to which he could be restored if the bishop or priest to whom he was entrusted like a prisoner on parole testified that he had performed his penance well, and on the condition that he made satisfaction to the relatives of the slain by playing a son's part and saying, "Whatever you want, I will do it for you." But if he did not make satisfaction, he was to remain in perpetual exile, a wanderer and a fugitive on the earth like Cain. In this penance there was an opportunity of social redemption; one could fulfil the conditions and return. But for the layman who perjured himself out of greed, there was nothing so comparatively lenient. He who had asked God to witness a lie was called on to sell all his property, give the proceeds to the poor, receive the tonsure, bid farewell to the whole world, and serve God in a monastery until death. The only leniency in the canon concerning perjury arises out of a recognition of possible causes. If a man perjures through fear of death, he must do penance on bread and water for three years in unarmed exile, and for two more years he must abstain from wine and meat, and offering a life for himself, *animam pro se reddens,* he must free a slave or a bondmaid from the yoke of slavery; furthermore, he must give alms for yet two more years, abstaining from meat only; and in the seventh year let him communicate.

Such are the more extreme forms of the penances im-

posed for major sins in Columban's *Penitential*. They give
us an indication of how Columban and his priests dealt
with some of the penitents who travelled for pardon from
court and villa, farmstead and town. As he listened to their
sins and stood in Christ's place, he cannot ever have known
that this system of penance, created in part by the fathers in
Ireland and in part by himself, would have a greater and
more lasting influence upon the development of medieval
ecclesiastical institutions than his monastic rule. His *Penitential* is among the earliest codes known to have been used
in the West. In a most profound sense, he was *anam-chara*
to a whole long civilization.

Men and women came to him out of the turbulent kingdoms of the Franks so that the defaced image of God in
which they had been created might be renewed. There were
depths under depths of mystery in this image. He never professed to be a philosopher who could plumb the mystery
by verbal dialectic. The mystery silenced him. A silent
piety, he would write, is better and knows more than an
impious garrulity. Let men seek the supreme wisdom not
by verbal debate but by the perfection of a good life, a life
in which the divine image would shine out in splendour.
God the omnipotent, the invisible, the incomprehensible,
the ineffable, the unfathomable, when fashioning man out
of clay, ennobled him with the dignity of His image. "It is
a great dignity," said Columban, "that God bestowed on
man the image of His eternity and the likeness of His
character." He added that it was great damnation to defile
the image of God. The defilement filled him with such a
mind-retching disgust and revulsion that there is terror as
well as anger in the words he wrote about wretched man-

kind, inwardly rotten, full of bile, rheum, fluids, blood and phlegm, always stained and sullied by inner filth, suppurating, washed daily but daily polluted, cleaning and embellishing the corruptible body, and polluting and degrading what is splendid by nature. Perceiving the extremes to which his revulsion drives him, one begins to fear that he sees in matter nothing but defilement, but the fundamental Christian sanity in him remains sound. Wretched human nature is not wholly depraved. "The choice of free will, though beatitude be lost, is not lost." There is freedom to turn and love God, and love of God is restoration. Love of God is the renovation of His image. *Dei enim dilectis imaginis ejus renovatis.* There is freedom to walk the highway of life (one of his dominant metaphors) on which a whole lifetime is like the journey of a single day towards the fatherland where the Father is, towards the city of the living God: *ad civitatem Dei viventis.* But the journey is a battle, not a mere resolve. True love is not in word only, but in deed and truth. Yet human goodness is not strong enough for anyone to acquire by his own efforts alone what he lost in Adam. Call on God's grace; be as Christ; walk even as Christ walked; travel on with afflictions of the body, with toil and humility, with lawful duty performed, and with Christ's grace in faith, hope and charity.

Here, in the Sacrament of Penance which he and his priests administered, there was renovation of the image. And so Luxeuil became a place of pilgrimage for the sinners of the kingdoms.

CHAPTER 4

The Dark Easter

A MAN making and building can be a happy man. He creates according to the image in which he himself was created. There is a certain fulfilment of his nature. During all those busy years on the roads of Gaul, in Annegray, Luxeuil and Fontaines, Columban was making and building, but it was not part of his exile's wisdom that he should perceive how an exile, a stranger in a strange land, must come to some terms with strange customs and tongues and foreign temperament. For much that he had achieved, he must have had the approval of the bishops of Gaul who knew of his preaching, his monasteries, his school and his own life. Around and about the achievement, however, there were visible and challenging signs of his foreignness.

He had brought with him a regard for monastic institutions far higher than was held by many of the bishops of Gaul. Without, it seems, getting the authorization which he should have sought from the diocesan, he had established his monasteries in the diocese of Besançon. When the time came after those immense labours of clearing away rubble and building, when the time came for the consecration of the church of St. Peter in Luxeuil, it was an Irish

bishop who had performed the consecration. It was as if
Columban were not in Gaul but in Ireland. He and his
monks differed in tonsure and certain details of liturgical
practice from the monks and priests of Gaul. But this
"most tenacious follower of Irish traditions" was not in
Ireland, but in Gaul. That he was left alone to go his own
way for so long was probably the result of episcopal caution,
episcopal respect for his friendship with Burgundian
nobles and courtiers, and a genuine admiration for the
effects of his labours among the people.

There was silence, then, a long quietness as of breathless
autumn months in the twilit arcades of the forests before the storms burst and the wolves crouched in the brakes
and the squirrels scuttled from the pelting rain and birds
sang no more. He had lived too long, in companionship or
alone in solitary places, under the sky, not to be able to
read the weather-signs, the turn in the wind and fluttering
of leaves, the movement of clouds, the flawing of still
waters, the colours of the day's end and beginning, and the
changes on the face of the moon. Yet, it was the moon in
her courses across the night sky, filling that sylvan and
mountain landscape with a light like a powdering of frost,
that would bring him a great trouble, heartache, bitter controversy and anxiety. It was the same moon by which the
Jews reckoned time, as hung over the land of Egypt when
many centuries and empires ago the Lord spoke to Moses
and Aaron and through them commanded the whole en-
slaved people of Israel to sacrifice the lamb without blem-
ish, on the fourteenth day of the moon in the evening,
sprinkle the blood on doorways, jambs and lintels alike,
roast the flesh and eat it with unleavened bread and wild

herbs, every man prepared and girt for travelling with his staff in his hand. It was the night of the Pasch, the Lord's passing by, when the angel of death struck every first-born thing in Egypt so that while it was still the dead of night, Pharao and all the land rose in fear, and the next day Israel began the journey out of bondage. "You are to observe this day as a memorial of the past, a day when you keep holiday in the Lord's honour, generation after generation. . . ."

It was the old world, the old law, the ancient type of the new reality: Christ, the Paschal Lamb, was sacrificed; Christ, risen from the dead, delivered His people from the bondage of hell. It was the time of the Pasch and its ful-filment. But the old continued to harass the new, and the foreshadowing to shadow the figure, and in the dispute that arose between Jewish Christian and Gentile Christian about the commemoration of Christ's Death and Resurrec-tion there was the beginning of centuries of controversy, computations, passion, uncharitable conduct, conciliar edicts, near-schisms, and a wearying waste of words of which the most important, as Columban himself said, were not more important than the tiniest truth in the gospels. He argued about the computations. Vehemently, he engaged in the controversy as it was in his day and sent it back to Rome, where it had been so often before, pleading with the pope, the great Gregory, for a decision that would confirm him and the Irish in their belief and practice.

At least four centuries of controversialists had preceded him. When, was the ancient question, did the Paschal fast end; and men in the beginning looked to the moon, that poor mistress for measurement of time, for an answer. For the Jewish Christians who closely connected Christ with

the prefiguring Paschal Lamb, the fast ended at the same
time as that of the Jews, on the fourteenth day of the first
month, Nisan, at evening; and two days after, without regard to the day of the week, came the Easter festival. For
them the guiding principle was the day of the lunar
month. The Gentile Christians, however, cutting themselves away from the Judaizers, kept the first day of the
week as the feast of the Resurrection, and held the previous
Friday, no matter which day of the month it was, to com-
memorate the Crucifixion. For them, the guiding principle
was the day of the week. Lunar and solar computations
were being followed. It was soon evident that there would
be divergence when two days after the fourteenth moon
would not be the same as the first day of the week, nor two
days before the first day of the week the same as the fourteenth moon. The divergence was extended with the spread
of the Church until it might be said that generally the
East kept to the Jewish rule of the fourteenth day while
the West observed the first day of the week as the feast of
the Resurrection.

In the succeeding centuries these differences, and others
that were added by later computations, became the material
of the long-drawn-out debate in which pope, bishop, saint,
monk, astronomer and historian engaged, often with more
knowledge and dexterity than wisdom. Unity among Christians about the celebration of the major feast and pivotal
date of the liturgical year was desirable. But how was it to
be attained? In the second century St. Polycarp, Bishop of
Smyrna, travelled to Rome to persuade Pope Anicetus into
accepting the Eastern practice—whose followers were already being called Quartodecimans (*quartus decimus,*

fourteenth), a name that would in the future almost mean
heresy. "Polycarp," wrote Eusebius the historian, "was not
able to persuade the pope, nor the pope Polycarp, but the
bonds of charity were not broken." Hardly forty years later,
the spirit of the debate has changed, and a pope threatens
excommunication of those who rejected the Roman usage.
Presently, as other cycles were invented on a luni-solar
basis, the usages were called into question as were the
computations on which they were based.

Up and down Christendom there arose argument after
argument about the moon and the sun, the vernal equinox,
the 14th lunation of Nisan, coincidence with the Jews, and
the meaning of uniformity. Defective or inadequate science, a passionate desire for uniformity, and a deep respect
for the significance of Easter Day drove men to relentless,
wearying controversy. For a time, it seems, Rome and the
West, including Ireland and Britain, used a cycle of 84
years, Easter falling between March 25 and April 21, and
the 14th to the 20th of the moon. It was to this cycle and
to its results that the Irish would cling as to something ancient and right received with the Faith. In Alexandria and
the East, a different cycle, of 19 years, the Metonic or
Alexandrian, was used, and it made Easter fall between
March 22 and April 25 and the 15th and 21st of the moon.
Both cycles kept the rule of observing Easter Day on the
Sunday after the spring full moon. The disputes that arose
from the differences and the lack of uniformity in observance were among the reasons that brought about the
Council of Nicaea in 325.

It was the council's decision that Easter Day should be
kept on the same Sunday throughout the world. The cor-

rect date was to be calculated in Alexandria, city of the astronomers, and the bishop of Alexandria was to announce the date to the churches under his jurisdiction and also to the occupant of the Roman see. The intent of the decision was clear. The practical side was not. What authoritative rule was there by which the Paschal moon was to be ascertained?

Within the West itself there now occurred differences that gave the controversy fresh vitality. The West was reluctant to abandon the 84-year cycle, but about the middle of the fourth century Rome adopted a variant of the cycle which had solar limits for Easter between March 22 and April 21, and lunar limits between the 16th and 22nd. The object of not keeping Easter Day before the 16th lunation appears to have been to make it possible for Good Friday to fall on the 14th of Nisan, which was generally believed to have been the actual day of the Crucifixion; and so, Easter Day would be separated from the Jewish festival. The shadow of the quartodecimans could be alarming! The West was to see yet more changes.

In 457 Victorius of Aquitaine attempted to compose differences and reconcile the Roman and Alexandrian computations with a new cycle of 532 years, and the date of Easter Day now had solar limits of March 22 and April 24, and lunar limits of the 16th and 22nd. The Victorian cycle was not adopted in Italy. Less than seventy years later, Dionysius Exiguus, a monk in a Roman monastery, revised the Victorian cycle, and Easter Day was to fall on a Sunday between the 15th and the 21st of the moon, or March 22 and April 25. It was this cycle that St. Augustine and his disciples introduced, with difficulty, into Britain. For in the meantime, the Britons and the Irish had been holding faithfully to the older cycle which fixed the vernal equinox at March 25. According to the Celtic usage, Easter Day could never fall later than April 21. But by mathematics and misfortune, Easter Day coincided with the Jewish Pasch whenever the 14th of the moon fell on a Sunday. So, at frequent and regular intervals, the shadow of the Quartodecimans could fall on the Celtic faithful! In the years 596, 600 and 603, for instance, not only did the Irish worship with the Jews, but their Easter Day differed from the day observed in Gaul.

No history of the pullulating controversies, no matter how lucid, can make the long interlocked business other than a great weariness. Time seemed to luxuriate in a lush growth of computations like an impenetrable and frustrating thicket that could darken the light of eternity. There was futility and anger, with charity frequently forgotten, Christian bishop refusing to sit at the same table or eat in the same house with Christian bishop, like that Dagan, perhaps an Irishman, who shocked St. Augustine's successor, Archbishop Laurentius in Britain, with his incivility. Laurentius had heard of Columban's obstinacy in Gaul on the road from Rome. He probably learned about it from some of the Gallic prelates who resented not only the different and Quartodecimanian Easters but also the unique situation of this Irishman who founded monasteries without episcopal consent, ruled more than one community, made no reports, moved about as he pleased, and received gifts of property without permission—all in the teeth of Gallic conciliar decrees.

The storms were about to burst on the embowered and cloistered silence of Luxeuil. Columban would be in the heart of the storm. He himself would be part of the storm.

2

As far as Jonas the hagiographer is concerned, the winds might as well have never blown. Jonas is silent about the heartbreaking controversy to which the founder devoted so much energy, so many obstinate years, so much passion and so many pages of writing. Was it because Columban was wrong and was defeated? If he had been right and victorious, it is probable that Jonas would have memorialized his learning and his victory. Or was it because the controversy was less active when Jonas came to write, that the monks of Luxeuil had come to peace and conformity with the Gallic hierarchy, and that the monks of Bobbio, Jonas's monastic home, were specially favoured by the Holy See? It is likely. It is also likely that as he gathered the stories and the anecdotes for the writing of the life, he met old tonsured heads that bobbed and nodded in eager conversation about the great days of the founder and turned away to silence when once more the old Easter question was raised and one might hear, far off, the ominous growling of the Bear of Luxeuil rounding on his hunters.

The scandalized Gallic prelates, the hunters, had to proceed with circumspection against Columban. He was no ordinary, furtive and peccant priest to be pulled down in a day's run. They reported him to Candidus, who had come in 595 as rector of the papal patrimony in Burgundy where

Queen Brunhilde was still regarded by Pope Gregory as regent. Columban also resorted to Candidus but without much satisfaction. The bishops prepared for a public accusation. Their own ground in face of the Bear was not so safe. Some of them, as Pope Gregory had reminded them in his great impulse of ecclesiastical renovation, were simoniacal, and led immoral lives, and indeed, creatures such as the historian of Tours described, worldly men, drunkards, wenchers and devotees of venery, still existed. Columban and his monks were one of their signs of contradiction. Moreover, the Easter they observed was not the same as the Roman.

In the year of Our Lord, 600, Columban wrote to the Pope. His first words were like a greeting with thrown flowers. "To the Holy Lord and Father in Christ," he wrote —the translation is Walker's—"the fairest Ornament of the Roman Church, as it were a most honoured Flower of all Europe in her decay, to the distinguished Bishop, who is skilled in the meditation of divine Eloquence, I, bar-Jonah (a poor Dove), send greeting in Christ." It was not the first time or the last he would pun in Hebrew and Latin on his own name, Jonah, Columba, the Dove. As he continues, his tone becomes manly and weighty. He writes carefully and firmly, interweaving the word-order, using frequent alliteration, a few puns, and some peculiar words derived from Greek. He is a man who even in a passion of argument does not forgo his delight in words.

What, he asks the pope, have you to say about an Easter celebrated on the 21st or 22nd of the moon, which previously many toiling scholars have proved to be no Easter, considering the darkness? (The darkness oppresses him.

Easter is light, the shining white splendour of the Resurrection. This thought remains in his mind. It is more than a thought. It is a poetic realization. The Irish cycle prohibits the celebration after the 20th of the lunation so that the moon may yet be bright.) In favour of his contention, he cites as authority the bishop of Syrian Laodicea, Anatolius, who had, he claimed with certainty, written against such an Easter in which the moon's rising is delayed until the middle of the night when light does not prevail over darkness, but darkness over light. It is sad to say that Columban cited, not Anatolius, but an Irish forgery which he had accepted as authentic. He quoted further from the forgery to declare that those who decided on such an Easter were without scriptural authority and could incur the charges of sacrilege and contumacy, with peril to their souls.

Next, he denounced the computations of Victorius of Aquitaine. Why, he asked the pope, why do you favour a dark Easter? He is surprised that the error has not been scraped away by the pope, like a warty growth, but he is ready to understand and excuse. Perhaps the pope is content with his predecessor's authority! But he must not be merely humble or seemly. For a living saint can right what by another and greater one has not been righted: *vivus namque sanctus emendare potest quae ab altero majore emendata non fuerint*. Gregory must be told that Victorius has not been accepted by Columban's teachers, the scholars of Ireland, and by the mathematicians most skilled in reckoning chronology but is more worthy of laughter and indulgence than respect. The scorn is quick and cutting. Wherefore, he begs Gregory for the support of his judg-

ment and for the timely mark of his approval "for the quell-
ing of this storm that surrounds us." He is not satisfied,
after much study, with the single judgment of those bishops
who can only say: We ought not to celebrate Easter with
the Jews. What, he asks sharply, has this to do with the case?
Is one to believe that the Jews, who crucified Christ and are
now without a temple, hold Easter? Is one to believe that
the Easter of the fourteenth moon is rightly theirs? As he
continues, preparing once more for a condemnation of
Victorius, he recollects who and what he is, and to whom he
writes; "For it befits neither place nor station that your
great authority should be at all questioned by the appearance of debate, and that you, who indeed lawfully occupy
the chair of Peter the apostle and bearer of the keys, should
ludicrously be troubled about Easter by my letters from the
West."

The apology is both an act of humility and a declaration
of belief in the supremacy of the throne of Peter. It was
uttered from something more profound and more important than ecclesiastical politeness. It was uttered out of that
tremendous central sanity which, even in the worst and
most acrimonious decades of controversy when men's
minds were addled with whirling computations and im-
agined heresies, sought for a most precious reality. Those
indefatigable debaters sought to end the scandal of dis-
unity, to bring about unity though they confused it with
uniformity, because the members of Christ are, and must
be, one.

Members of Christ? With the principle in mind, he
turns from the Easter question to the problem of simoniacal bishops in Gaul. "Is one," he asks, "to communicate

with them?" The question does not come from himself alone. He has been presented with the problem by some ecclesiastics in Gaul "whose confessions I have heard on this." They wished to know for certain whether after buying orders for money and secretly renouncing celibacy they could, *sine periculo,* without peril, become bishops.

He has other problems, and if physical weakness and the care of his fellow pilgrims, *meorum cura comperegrinorum,* had not kept him tied at home, he would follow his desire to go to Rome and speak to the pope himself. He has read one of Pope Gregory's books containing the pastoral rule and has found the work sweeter than honey to the needy. Will Gregory, therefore, send him the tracts which he has composed with wonderful skill upon Ezekiel? There are other writings of Gregory he wishes to have as well. And asking pardon for the roughness of his letter, he prays for peace for the pope and begs for his prayers. In the final sentence he refers again to Easter: "And if, as I have heard from holy Candidus your officer, you wish to make this reply, that what has been confirmed by long passage of time cannot be changed, clearly the error is of long standing; but truth has always stood longer, and is its refutation."

We do not know if the messenger who set out with the letter from Luxeuil, and perhaps with other writings of Columban's about the Easter question, ever reached Rome and Pope Gregory. It was a long and dangerous road, especially through Italy, where the Lombard invasions had unsettled life. Other letters of Columban's were lost on the same roads. At any rate, if Gregory received the letter and did reply, we have no knowledge of it.

The case was neither won nor finished. As far as Colum-

ban and the Gallic bishops were concerned, it was only beginning. They continued to work against him. He continued to celebrate Easter in his fashion, so that in 602 he
celebrated a week earlier than the rest of Gaul and in 603
on a date which coincided once more with the Jewish
Pasch.

3

For strategical purposes, the bishops were on firmer
ground than they had been in the days of Gunthram and
of his nephew Childebert II who had ruled both Burgundy and Austrasia. Childebert had died in 596, having
failed to keep in check the ambitious counts and dukes
who lusted for power. His two infant sons, Theudebert
and Theuderich, had been left to the care of their grandmother, the ageing unconquerable Brunhilde, who had to
protect them against the same old lusts and ambitions. But
once again, the divisionary Merovingian principle was at
work. Theudebert, the elder, became ruler of Austrasia,
and Theuderich ruler of Burgundy. In this division of
power and in its consequent weakening, the terrible Queen
Fredegund, whose intrigues had never ceased, now saw her
opportunity, as regent for her son Clothair, to urge Neustria into war against her great-nephews. The unwearying
bloody Frankish swords were drawn. At Lafaux, near Laon,
Theudebert and the Austrasians were heavily defeated and
all the lands as far as the Meuse fell to Fredegund. What
she had failed to attain by conspiracies, assassinations and
bribes, now seemed almost hers: that she, and her young

son born fatherless, should rule all and humble Brunhilde and those who had ever scorned her. Then, in Rouen, she died, this servant-woman who by carnality and indefatigable cunning had played such deadly games with kings and kingdoms. She reached a quieter deathbed than fortune had in store most terribly for Brunhilde.

Fredegund's death brought no peace to that poor queen. The hideous years that had passed since she came out of Spain, young, very beautiful, good-living, intelligent and loved, to marry Sigibert, had pressed upon her intolerably: husbands and sister murdered, perpetual peril to her life and her son's, attempted assassinations, conspiracies against her spun out in a far-reaching web by Fredegund and by enemy nobles. There was left nothing of the bright girlhood that Venantius Fortunatus had celebrated as a splendour of roses and lilies to dim the lustre of sapphire, diamonds, crystal and pearls. She had had to learn the grim habit of fighting desperately for mere survival.

After the death of Fredegund, this fight became more intense. Ambitious nobles of Austrasia conspired against Brunhilde. She frustrated one plot. Another succeeded. In the year 599, they rose armed against her and she had to flee alone from Metz. She was lucky to escape with her life to Burgundy where, received with honour, she took refuge with Theuderich, the younger of her grandsons.

She was fortunate, too, in that the mayor of the palace, a Gallo-Roman, assisted her in upholding the royal authority in Burgundy. She needed the expert help. The young King Theuderich, no more than a boy, was a weak vessel of authority both by his age and his inexperienced nature. He was a true Merovingian. He also could be moved by sudden

religious impulses. He frequently rode to Luxeuil to visit
Columban and to ask for his prayers. It is doubtful if he
understood much of that creative monastic effort, but at
least he could always count on a father's blessing from the
abbot. If, at times, the father was frostily stern, there was
good reason. Theuderich was precociously a sexual ad-
venturer like so many of his ancesters. Already he was
keeping concubines and begetting children. In the year
602-603, a second bastard son was born to him.

It is probable that in self-indulgence he had gone beyond
the old queen's control, or indeed beyond any control that
would interfere with his strong desires. Conscious of Merovingian wilfulness of which she had had bitter experience,
she may have looked away from his scandalous adventures,
biding her time, choosing between evils, and gone on with
the daily burdensome business of trying to govern and keep
the royal power intact. She did, indeed, wish he were married, fathering true heirs. Whatever her part was, it was
obscure. She has had her vindicators who have depicted her
as a wronged and most Christian woman. And she has had
her detractors. A chronicler of the time, Fredegarius, described her, in effect, as a wicked old schemer who aided
her grandson in his debauchery so that she might be free
to rule. Nor does Jonas spare her. He writes of her un-
sympathetically as a woman into whom the ancient serpent
had entered, a second Jezabel.

It must be remembered that Jonas was no calm, judicial
historian. Brunhilde had quarrelled with Columban; and
Columban had thundered against her. That was enough
for him. Columban was right. She was wrong. He knew
only of the violent conflict between the queen and his

saintly founder. Besides, there was the fact of her brutal
death like the judgment of an angry God.

Because she was a Christian woman, she cannot but
have admired the labours of Columban and his monks.
There were physical evidences of those labours for her to
see in the flowering reclaimed lands and in the monastery
buildings risen from secular ruins. She cannot but have
approved in her conscience of whatever spiritual influence
he sought to exercise over her grandson, a mere boy among
his concubines. Yet, something happened between herself
and the abbot to diminish the charity in their relationship.
Jonas would attribute it to her wickedness. Wickedness or
not, her possible patronage of Columban was not forth-
coming in the next stage of the quarrel about the date
of Easter with the bishops.

At this time there was in Vienne a bishop named Desiderius. He was a man in temper and courage very like the
abbot of Luxeuil. He worked zealously against simony and
loose living among his brother prelates and priests and
against the profligacy of the Burgundian court. Inevitably
he made enemies, but their existence troubled his sense of
duty very little and in the end he would die violently, a
martyr, at their hands. He, like Columban, remonstrated
with Theuderich, and more than likely with the regent
Brunhilde. Somewhere among his enemies, a person was
found to bring against him the charge of adultery on the
evidence of a trollop. He was called on to meet the charge
before a council summoned to meet at the Burgundian
capital, Chalon on the Saône, in 603. A chronicler would
detect in this summons both the hand of Brunhilde, whose
profligate grandson had been reproached, and the hand of

Arigius, appointed in that year to the see of Lyons, who became at once a leader of the Gallic bishops. Arigius, it seems, also wrote to Columban, demanding that he justify himself in many matters before the council. Columban refused to attend. Was not Arigius Brunhilde's favourite? What Brunhilde resented, Arigius would resent. Columban's probable lack of confidence in the council's mercy was borne out by the fate of Desiderius, who was found guilty and banished from his see to a river-island. Banishment would be his fate too.

He had already written privately to Arigius, but the letter is lost. Now he wrote not only to Arigius but to their lordships on the council, and he wrote simply and forcefully, putting aside the civilized flourishes which, in the congeniality of friendship, one man might offer to another. The words of the Bible flow into the sense of what he says like sap into the branches of a tall tree that the storm can only shake.

Columba, the sinner, greets the bishops and priest in Christ and thanks God that for his sake "so many holy men have been gathered together to treat of the truth of faith and good works," and to judge of the matters under dispute "with a just judgment." With a hint of irony, he exclaims: "Would that you met more often!" He asks God to help them not only in their treatment of the Easter business, which has already been discussed at length and long decided in diverse ways by different authorities, but also in canonical observances, which have been corrupted by many men. Quoting St. Paul and the Evangelists, Matthew, Luke and John, he affirms that he who believes in Christ ought also himself to walk as Christ walked. The voice of the shepherds must be exemplified in their own practice. Therefore, let all together, clergy and monks, live according to the true and unique rules of our Lord Jesus Christ and thereafter, without pride, seek to record a unanimous verdict on the rest. By such living, the sons of God will enjoy among themselves true peace and full charity.

Peace and charity are the very ground of this letter. The two words recur as though he feared charity were dead and peace broken.

He observes that harm has been done to the peace of the Church by differences and diversities, but by living according to our Saviour, bishops and monks with hatred rooted out can love one another. In this spirit, the problem of Easter may be faced and the truth about the correct tradition—that of Gaul or of "your brothers in the West," *fratrum vestrorum in Occidente*—may be sought. He reminds them that in his writings he has stated his own conviction. He pleads with Bishop Arigius to bear with his ignorance in peace and charity, even with what some people have called the proud impudence of his writing. For necessity, not pride, has provoked him. Since he is not the author of the difference in observance, and has entered these lands as a pilgrim, he begs that he may be allowed with their lordships' peace and charity "to enjoy the silence of these woods and to live beside the bones of our seventeen dead brethren" as he has been allowed to live for twelve years till then.

In a beaten humiliated man, the plea would be pathetic and pitiful. But Columban as he writes—how many pages has he filled in all this business!—is not grovelling. He

carries himself with ursine majesty. He suspects the hunters
are surrounding him with nets and cords, but they must
first hear him.

He writes a lapidary sentence which, in the Latin, is very
memorable. *Capiat nos simul oro Gallia:* five words that
might be a proverb: Let Gaul, I beg, hold us side by side.

He knows, he says, that this verbosity of his will seem
excessive, but he thinks it right that the assembled bishops
should know what the monks in his monasteries are dis-
cussing and pondering among themselves. The rules they
live by, they have brought from their native land; they are
their arms, their shield and sword; and they pray and hope
that they will continue to wield them till death as they
have seen their predecessors do. Better for their lordships
to comfort rather than to confound these poor veterans and
aged pilgrims.

He next tells the members of the council that he does not
appear before them because he might strive with words and
be quarrelsome. In this judgment on himself he is right.
Thinned to the bone by his years of austerity, he still has
the old native fire burning in him. It is with the deep conviction of his conscience that he believes in the Easter tradition of his native land. But let their lordships choose
what they prefer to follow. Quoting St. Paul, he says, "Yet
you must scrutinize it all carefully, retaining only what is
good." Far be it from him that he should keep up the
quarrel and make their enemies, the unchristened, rejoice.
He and the bishops may agree in some way, so that both
sides, if both traditions are good, may remain as they were,
or so that a solution in agreement with Scripture may be
achieved and maintained.

Then, he uses ominous words.

If, he says, it is God's will that they should drive him
from his place of seclusion which he has sought from the
sea for the sake of Jesus Christ, then it will be his part to
speak prophetically: "If on my account this storm is upon
you, take me and cast me into the sea, that this tempest may
recede from you in calm." He, the Dove, quotes from the
book of Jonas the Prophet whose name, as he has punned
so often, also means dove. Let the bishops, like the sailors
in the Old Testament narrative, first try to save the ship-
wrecked by drawing the ship towards land: "And the men
sought to return to land and could not, for the sea ran
and the swell increased the more." But he does not continue the story about how the sailors took Jonas and threw
him over the ship's side! He spoke indeed prophetically by
a prophet. He was yet to be jettisoned.

He now nears the end of his letter, but he will have a
long last word in which he will reproach sinful ecclesiastics
and defend monasticism. Recalling the Scribes and Phari-
sees who shut the kingdom of heaven before men, he tells
their lordships that they should help, not hinder, those
souls who hasten towards the strait and narrow gate.
Heaven can be entered by those who become as little
children, humble, chaste, simple-hearted and guileless in
evil, but it can hardly be entered by those who lust after
women and more often dispute in anger over the riches of
the world. The monks cut off the causes of such sins by renouncing the world and living in naked poverty. A child is
humble, forgets injury, does not lust after a woman when
he sees her, and does not keep one thing on his lips and
another in his heart. Such virtue will be better preserved

"by one who is still and sees that God Himself is Lord, than by one who sees and hears all manner of things."

He is defending the detachment that is the basis of his asceticism: the stillness of the spirit, "for unless they grow lukewarm, cloistered men live better than public men, except for that even more austere life which has the greater reward"—which may have been an allusion to Gregory the Great who remained a monk while active as the pope, the most public figure in Christendom. St. Jerome commanded bishops to imitate the Apostles, but he taught monks to follow the fathers who were perfect. "For the patterns for clergy are one thing, and for monks another, and widely separated from one another." But let each hold to what he has taken; and let all maintain the gospel, and both parties, like harmonious parts of one body, follow Christ by His own commands which were revealed by Him to be fulfilled "in charity and peace." The words recur now in sentence after sentence as, with a prayer, the letter moves to its conclusion: "For the rest, fathers, pray for us as we also pray for you, wretched though we be, and do not count us estranged from you, for we are members of one body, whether Gauls, or Britons, or Irish, or whatever our race. . . ."

We do not know what the council thought of this letter. All we know is that it did not take action against its author. For yet awhile, he was granted the peace and charity he had begged for, and he could go on living in the silence of the woods beside the bones of his dead brethren. He had not given up hope of a decision in Rome on the Easter question, though letters he had written had come back because the bearers failed or were unable to travel the war-troubled

roads of Italy. We do know from his own words in another
letter he wrote to Rome that he was fearful of his opponents, who indulged "more in raising disturbances against
him than in reasoned arguments."

It was in the next year, 604, when the Irish monks and
Gaul again celebrated Easter at different dates, that he
wrote this letter. It was not a year for peace of mind. One
of the young King Theuderich's concubines gave birth to
a son, a third royal cause of scandal in the eyes of Columban. In March of the same year, the "servant of the servants
of God," Pope Gregory the monk, died in ill-health of
mind and body in Rome. As much as anybody, Columban
must have realized that one of the giant creative Christian
founders had worked himself to death in teaching and re-
forming Christendom and extending its frontiers, in performing vast methodical works of charity, in enlarging the
power of the papacy, and in defending Rome itself against
the Arian Lombards. In Columban's lifetime there had
been six popes, and now he wrote to the seventh whose
name he did not yet know, saying that for long his spirit
had desired the consolation of a visit to each occupant of
the apostolic see and that the wars of the age and the
turbulent treasons of the heretical races had prevented him.
To his comparatively brief letter, rather too stylishly composed, he attached the letters which the bearers had failed
to bring to Pope Gregory of blessed memory. It is again
the dispute about Easter that forms the matter of his message. The attached letters are to be taken as a demonstra-
tion of his people's belief in the Trinity—that if it be not
contrary to faith, he and his monks may be allowed to hold
the rite of Easter in the manner they had received from

their predecessors. "For it is agreed," he writes, "that we are in our native land."

The assertion illuminates Luxeuil and Annegray and Fontaines through all the millenary obscurity. They are not existing by the rules of Gaul. By diplomatic immunity, they are more than embassies. They are colonies, dwelling in seclusion, harming no one, abiding by the monastic way of life brought from Bangor. They do not come under the jurisdiction of the bishops of Gaul. The idea is strong and clear in Columban's mind as he concludes the letter with a reminder to the pope that there is conciliar authority for preserving this immunity. As Columban sees it, the one hundred and fifty authorities of the Council of Constantinople, which met in 381, decreed that the churches of God set up among pagan peoples, *in barbaris gentibus,* should live by their own laws as taught them by their fathers.

It is not the letter of a man without deep anxieties. There is a storm roaring intermittently around his seclusion, and it is not going beyond the evidence to deduce that he feels insecure and fears he and his people may not weather it. In hardly more than another year, a new storm comes from another direction and threatens his work with ruin.

4

In a sense, Columban was himself the author of the storm that finally darkened life in Luxeuil.

Being what he was and believing as he did, he could not do otherwise than attempt to reclaim King Theuderich from the concubines. He took to task the royal visitor to the monastery and counselled marriage so that the royal house would then derive, not from harlots, but from an honourable queen. There was even more need for Columban's stern interference. In the year 606-607, Theuderich had begotten another illegitimate son.

Moves had already been made to have him married, and it is almost certain that the old Queen Brunhilde, whom Jonas depicts as a scheming Jezabel, desired the marriage and worked for it. The choice of wife was Ermenberg, daughter of Betterich, the king of the Visigoths. Bishop Arigius fetched her out of Spain. It may be true that Brunhilde, as Jonas says, feared that her own honours and dignities would be diminished if a new queen ruled the court and the concubines were put away. It may be also true that when she saw the young Spanish princess married to her grandson and the concubines still in attendance, she despaired of bringing sanity into the Merovingian madness. Fredegarius the chonicler blames her for what happened to Ermenberg. The marriage was never consummated. In hardly more than a year the young girl was sent back to Spain, robbed of the treasures she had brought with her: this, despite the oath given to Betterich that she would not be put away. The political consequences were more important than even old Queen Brunhilde expected. Betterich leagued with King Clothair of Neustria, King Theudebert of Austrasia, and with Agilulf, king of the Lombards (Columban would yet meet him), for an attack on the kingdom of Burgundy. The attack did not take place, but Burgundy was in danger, and Theudebert would later invade Alsace.

The scandal of Theuderich's life was more than Columban could tolerate. In his letter to the pope who succeeded Gregory and whose name he did not know, he had claimed immunity under a canon of the Council of Constantinople from interference by the bishops of Gaul. In this matter of the young scandalous king, he should have, in reason, allowed their lordships the same freedom in their affairs from interference by Columban. The conduct of King Theuderich was certainly their affair. Was not Bishop Arigius a close friend of Queen Brunhilde and a leader of their lordships? Surely he could say what was needful! Columban must have thought that what ought to be said and done was not being said or done. In any case, it is more than likely that what he intended as charity towards the young king was also an expression of strong paternal affection.

One day, therefore, as Jonas tells, he went to see Queen Brunhilde. She was then staying with the king's illegitimate children at the villa of Bourcheresse, situated halfway between Chalon-sur-Saône and Autun. This Gallo-Roman villa, pillared and porticoed, spacious, floored with tesselated pavements and surrounded in a quiet green valley by elaborate gardens, was the favourite of the numerous royal residences. When the queen saw Columban entering the main hall of the villa she led forward the four children, the youngest hardly more than two years old, to meet this emaciated figure that stood staff in hand, solemn, perhaps even grim, and most certainly unsmiling. That he had come at all to see her, and that she led the children forward, suggests that there had been some sort of friendly relations between them. His first question gives a hint of his mood. He asked what did the children want.

"They are the king's sons," she replied. "Strengthen them with your blessing."

In the request and in his answer, there came one of the turning-points in his life. What she asked for was ostensibly very little to ask from a man who blessed abundantly men and fields, doorways, food and the spoon with which he supped. A hand lifted ritually, the mind for an instant intent, words murmured in the name of the Trinity. The children, bastards though they were, were innocent of their father's guilt. Commentators have professed, however, to discern the true motives in the queen's heart and to read in her words an effort to gain before the courtiers the approbation of the powerful abbot of Luxeuil for the king's sons, one of whom might be heir. It seems that Columban interpreted her request in that manner, for his disastrous reply was harsh.

"You must know," he said, "that these will never hold the royal sceptre, because they came from the brothel."

Furious, the old queen told the children to leave. Columban, apparently, turned and walked out of the palace. There was terror in the house.

Had Columban travelled the miles of road and paths between Luxeuil and the villa just for this wrathful, prophetic retort to a woman who had asked that her great-grandchildren might be strengthened by his blessing? Perhaps after long meditation he had decided that it was time to shock her and, through her, the young king into an awareness of Christian responsibility. He left terror behind him, and Jonas hints at a miracle, because the whole house shook as the abbot crossed the threshold. Whatever was

the meaning he intended to give the encounter, it marked
the beginning of the queen's active enmity.

Terror left her anger unaffected. She began to lay plans
against him. Messengers were sent to those of the king's
subjects living near the monastery with orders to prevent
the monks from leaving the monastic enclosure, to stop
supplies of food or help to them and to refuse all contact.
These were the first moves in the siege.

They were more than Columban expected—which does
suggest that his harsh words had, paradoxically, been uttered in the familiarity of friendship. When he realized
how the royal anger was directed against him, he hastened
back along the roads to try and turn aside the obstinate
woman's intent by treating with the king. Already, going
hard, he had been marching for at least a fortnight; and
now, returning to save his monks and his monasteries, he
had a longer march, across valley after valley until he was
in the ancient high Celtic country where Vercingetorix
had been defeated by Caesar. His destination was the king's
palace at Epoisses, near Semur-en-Auxois.

It was near sunset when he reached the palace gates. The
king was told that he had arrived but that he refused to
cross the threshold. This refusal to accept the hospitality of
the house was an old form of protest that would have been
understood in Gaul as in Ireland. It struck at something
primal and sacred. There was injustice under the roof-tree.
Let it be put right. Columban now gave it scriptural sanc-
tion as well, quoting from Ecclesiasticus.

King Theuderich said to his courtiers: "It is better to
pay due honour to the man of God, rather than to provoke
the Lord's anger by offending His servants."

He, therefore, ordered that a royal feast be prepared and sent to the servant of God. Then the servants came with the feast and Columban looked at the regal food and goblets and asked what it all meant.

"The king ordered them to be brought to you," they said.

Spurning the offering, he said: "It is written: The Most High approveth not the gifts of the wicked. It is not fitting that the lips of the servants of God should be defiled by the food of him who denies them entry not only to his own home but to the homes of other men."

It is not quite clear in Jonas what happened next. At any rate, the goblets were all smashed and the wine and other drinks scattered with the food on the ground. It is clear that the servants were terrified and that their terror was communicated to the king. He and his grandmother, Brunhilde, hastened to the man of God, asked his pardon and promised to emend what was wrong. Pacified by these promises, Columban took the road back to the monastery.

It was only a temporary victory. The encounter had been terrifying, but when the abbot was gone back to his monastery, Theuderich went on living his disorderly life as if nothing had happened. When the news reached Columban, he took pen and parchment and wrote a letter, now lost, in which he scourged the king and the queen with reproaches and threatened excommunication if they delayed any longer in the emendation of their lives.

It is probable that if he had only the king to deal with, he might have achieved some measure of reform, even without the threat of excommunication which, in his condition as abbot without jurisdiction in a professedly insulated monastery, he had no power to make effective. But he was also dealing with a woman whom he had insulted into wrath before her great-grandchildren and the courtiers in the villa at Bourcheresse. Life had made her implacable in her designs. And her design now was to destroy the immunity in which the monastery of Luxeuil existed. The storm was about to blow full force after many premonitions.

She again set about rousing the king against Columban, and she asked all the courtiers and nobles to help her. It was an easy task. The king's own sensual nature was in league with her, resentful of any inhibitions that the abbot might try to impose on him. She was not content, however, to rely on arousing the king's antipathy. She approached the bishops, probably through Arigius, and attacked what they had already been assembled to criticize, that is, the mode of life in the monastery and the rule Columban imposed on his monks. In this matter, half the battle was won for her. This alien monastic island with its strange tonsure, liturgy, customs, its different liturgical calendar and its immunity from the power of the diocesan, was a reproach to the ineffectiveness of the hierarchy. The courtiers, who included ecclesiastics, joined with the queen in turning the king's mind against the abbot and persuading him that he should investigate Luxeuil. So, the wretched young man rode out with his followers to confront Columban.

He was not the best-equipped of visitors. His mentors had primed him with questions, foolish questions that were directed by malice and towards the deformation of the monastery. He, or they, had also formed a plan by which they would dispose of the monk and his closest followers.

For nearly twenty years Luxeuil, and indeed the other monasteries, had been building an island of quietness, physical and spiritual quietness, in the desolation. Where there had been the rank and riotous confusion of vegetation and broken walls, there was now physical order, the cells, the chapel, the refectory, guest house and other buildings standing in their necessary arrangement. The enclosure pushed off the world, cut it away and apart from these men who desired only to pray in the manner they had learned from the Irishman: the Mass, the Divine Office, the hymns, the study of Sacred Scripture and the Fathers; work in the fields, the forest, and at building. The enclosure might as well have been the high mounds of Irish earth, ditched at the base and firm against the weather with grass, that surrounded the secluded human habitations in Ireland, and the sky might as well have been the Irish sky over Bangor or Clonard or the islands in Lough Erne. Except that the world, year after year, had sent men and women, nobles and courtiers, landowners, farmers and their workers, to confess their sins, eat and sleep in the guest house, make their peace, and find themselves in the silence as many strangers have found their neglected true selves in monasteries. They accepted the silence; they came in quietness. Now their king rode in with his men, armed worldly men who loved war, the chase, great feasts of meat and wines, and women. Their horses and the jingle of the ornamented accoutrements and loud voices filled the streets of the monastery.

Where exactly the king and Columban met, Jonas does not say; but one gets the impression of prying and movement among the buildings. The king questioned the abbot about why he had departed from the customs of the province and why entry was not given to all Christians into the more secluded parts of the monastery. The imputation of something sinister to monastic privacy is one of the perennial practices of antipathetic rulers. Young Theuderich, who had frequently visited the monastery, must have well known what was here and what was there and why. Courageously and vigorously, the abbot replied that it was not his custom to allow outsiders and people of the world to enter the living quarters of God's servants, and that fit and proper places had been provided for all such guests.

The king replied, with more than a hinted threat: "If you wish to retain the gifts of our generosity and our full support, you must give free entry to all parts of the monastery."

The direction of his talk with the abbot had been well planned. The answer he received was inevitable.

"If you attempt to violate what has been set up here until now by the rule of discipline, neither your gifts nor your help will ever be accepted by me. And if this be the cause of your coming to this place, that you would destroy the cloisters of God's servants and defile the rule of discipline, I say to you that soon your kingdom will be destroyed and all your race scattered."

By this time, the king had entered the refectory, a place forbidden to people of the world. Columban's words—prophetic, as they were to prove—struck on all his fears like a hammer on a gong. Hastily, he turned and left. Columban followed, still upbraiding him. After so many decades of assassinations and killings by which kings and princes died, it was not hard to make Merovingian memories and anxieties merge into terror. The king recovered himself and uttered a taunt: "You hope to gain through me the martyr's crown."

He went on to say that he was not so daft as to commit such a crime, and now the plan that had been prepared was announced. It was, in fact, the purpose of the royal visit. Those in the monastery who wished to segregate themselves from all the customs of the world should now return by the road to the place from which they had come. All the king's followers joined in crying together that they would not have among them in these places men who refused to associate with all others. What the king had pronounced and what the courtiers had supported with a hound-pack babel of sound was a sentence of banishment. This was the real breaking of the silence of Luxeuil.

Columban replied that he would not leave the monastery enclosure unless he were dragged from it by force.

Did he hope that his person, as abbot, would be respected? Did he imagine that these Frankish men, pious, superstitious, violent in their impulses and volatile, would be content with this show of force and leave the monastery in a state of anxiety and secular siege? He cannot have had any such comfort. That taunt about the martyr's crown had a sinister meaning from a recent event. It was only a short time since Bishop Desiderius of Vienne had, by royal blundering or by royal design, been beaten to death by a stone and a club in a place to which he had been dragged by soldiers.

The king rode away from the monastery, and what he had come to do was done. He left behind him with some of his followers one Count Baudulf who took Columban by force and led him "in exile," as Jonas puts it, to the city of Besançon. He had no company of his own except the young man, Domoal.

It is likely that the king had wavered at the last minute in carrying out his plan for banishing all those monks back to the place from which they had come. He may have expected that this show of force, this forceful carrying of Columban to Besançon, would cool the prophetic abbot's ardour and make him more amenable, while the monks at Luxeuil, now without their founder, would become cowed. But Columban could no more remain still than he could cast off his habit and his way of life.

5

Once a provincial capital, Besançon had become a fortress and prison city. It had been built by the Romans on the high and commanding head of land around which the river Doubs flows in a sweep that almost brings it back on its own course. Columban heard that the prison was full of condemned men who awaited execution. He went, freely it seems, and preached to the condemned men who lay there fettered in irons. It would have been unlike him and out of harmony with the amplitude of his charity if he did not also care for their physical needs in whatever way he and Domoal could. The prisoners promised him that if they were set free, they would amend their lives and do penance for their misdeeds. There is a childlike innocence in the manner in which Columban is described by Jonas as accepting their promise, as if condemned men, criminals, had only to say they would be good so as to go free. He ordered Domoal to take hold of the iron that bound the

fetters together and to pull it. Domoal gripped the iron and
pulled, and it was shattered into pieces like a rotten twig.
Next, with their broken fetters off, Columban washed the
feet of the prisoners and dried them with a towel, as Christ
washed the feet of his Apostles. He bade them leave the
prison and go to the church, where they were to wash away
their guilt with repentance and tears. They went and found
the doors of the church locked.

In the meantime, the captain of the guard had discovered
the escape, the empty prison and the broken fetters, and in
these things he saw the power of God working through the
monk, Columban. Like a man risen from sleep, he went in
pursuit with his soldiers.

Then there was enacted a brief, dramatic and memorable scene that might have formed a subject for one of those
devotional panels carved in low relief in ivory which later
Frankish artists fashioned with such care and joy for the
sides of caskets or for the covers of sacred books: of Our
Lady ascending into heaven, and St. Gall offering bread
to a bear, as in the ivory cover of the *Evangelium Longum;*
or a saint and his followers baptizing a heathen king, the
lines of drapery and of the trees all stylized, the human
heads tilted together towards a central point.

Columban and Domoal have followed the prisoners towards the door of a church in the old city. There beneath
the arched portals the fugitives stand grouped, a sheaf of
lean ragged wretches just released from misery; they press
against the resisting timbers of the door in their urgent
need of sanctuary. The soldiers are now in the street, a
group of men running with spears and swords slanted
forward, led by a captain still dazed by the surprise of what

he has seen. The prisoners turn and implore Columban, who is some distance from the door, to rescue them from the danger. The abbot raises his eyes heavenwards and prays God not to let those he has just delivered from the fetters to fall once more into the hands of the soldiers.

The event must have been intolerably exciting. Almost in any second of its converging dramatic movements, it could be caught and held in the warm white of ivory in a perpetual memorial. Columban's forced sojourn in Besançon cannot have been very long. Yet this scene, brief though it must have been, was remembered most vividly during many decades until Jonas the monk came to write it down from, it is probable, the story as told by Domoal. Columban prays. The strong locks of the church spring open. The fugitives surge in. Behind them the doors swing shut against the soldiers as if, writes Jonas who is in his miraculous element, "some porter had promptly unlocked and locked them with a key." As Columban and Domoal reach the portals, the captain and his soldiers arrive. They call and search for the sexton. Even his name, Aspasius, will be recorded. He finds the keys, tries to open up, fails, and then remarks that he has never known the doors to be so securely fastened.

"After that," Jonas relates dryly, "no one dared lay a hand on those whom Providence had set free."

The writ of King Theuderich ran in Besançon, but it cannot have run very vigorously. This old Gallo-Roman city, Vesontio, was like other cities of the kind not quite under the full dominion and influence of the Franks. Among the Christian population, the municipal officials, the lawyers, merchants and traders, the artificers, and espe-

cially among the clerics, there would have been some of
the common cultural and social contempt for the barbarians who were still learning what was left of Roman laws,
manners, customs and urbanity. The contempt was to
Columban's advantage. Besides, his fame as a holy man was
known. After the affair of the prisoners he himself noticed
that he was no longer troubled by guards. They let him go
free about the streets of the high city that must have been
buzzing in every house, tavern and workshop, with stories
about the breaking of the fetters and the unlocking and
locking of the doors. Here surely was a man of God!
It would be prudent not to molest him for fear of sharing
in the guilt of his enemies. Let him walk wherever he
pleased.

But where he pleased was in that country within a country, his monastery, among his brethren. Although he was
free to wander the city, the road to Luxeuil was guarded, it
appears, against his escape. At least, it had been until one
Sunday morning when he climbed to one of the highest
points in the city, probably to the ramparts of the Roman
citadel on the hill, and looked out northeastwards across
the swirling river Doubs, the town gardens and fields, to
where the Roman road struck through the woods toward
Luxeuil. The road was empty. There were no guards to
hinder his going. He descended, and passing through the
centre of the city, crossed a bridge, and took the road back
to the monastery. The Dove returned to the nest. If the
monks rejoiced, it cannot have been from any sense of
confidence in the forbearance of the king and of Queen
Brunhilde.

CHAPTER 5

Exile within Exile

THE news of the unexpected return to Luxeuil must have reached the court with the speed of the wind. Whatever dilatory policy the king and queen had been practising up to this, it was now forced upon them to make a rapid and drastic decision about the abbot. He had flouted the royal command. Furious, Theuderich and Brunhilde ordered a company of soldiers to go to the monastery and bring him back to Besançon under duress, not for compulsory segregation but for the start of a journey he had long dreaded with prophetic foresight.

It is possible that the captain of the company of soldiers had heard of the events in Besançon. It is certain that he had less than half his heart in this sorry mission to lay violent hands on the ageing abbot. He had no intention, as Jonas writes, of injuring Columban. He may have been fearful through genuine reverence or through superstition, and in weighing the wrath of God for molestation of his servant against the wrath of the king for failure in duty, he may have decided not to find what he was sent to find. He and his soldiers arrived at the monastery and began their search for one monk out of scores of monks, habited alike,

wearing the same tonsure, and probably similar in measured gait and bearing from the formative discipline.
Columban was actually sitting in the porch of the church,
reading. He saw the soldiers pass close to him. Their boots
touched his sandals. They brushed against his habit. But
they did not see him. Jonas, filled with amazement, per-
ceives the miraculous, and says they could not see him although he was there to see. The captain himself came and,
looking through a window, saw Columban sitting unper-
turbed, reading at his ease as if the normal life of the
monastery were going on around him. For the captain the
failure of the searchers was a sign from heaven.

"Why," he called out to them, "are you searching the
porch of the church so carefully since you can find nothing
at all? Don't let his foolishness deceive you any further.
You'll never find the man who is hidden by God's power.
Give up. Let us hurry back to the king and tell him we
couldn't find him."

They returned and reported to an infuriated king, who
was now being made to appear ridiculous. He, however,
must have had very reliable information of the abbot's
presence in the monastery. On this occasion there would
be no blundering. He put one of his principal courtiers,
his chamberlain Count Bertechar, in charge of the operation, with Count Baudulf and a company of soldiers under
a captain named Ragamund—a man Columban would
come to know intimately during the month ahead. They
rode to the monastery to make a thorough and ruthless
search. When they had found the abbot they were to see
that a certain definite instruction was carried out to the
letter. All the many forces in Church and State that had

worked through many years against Luxeuil, its customs
and its separateness, and especially against the founder,
were gathered together in the determined energy of this
ride up through the forests.

There was no need to hunt through the enclosure for
the quarry. This was the end of the Merovingian hunt.
They rode in just at one of the Hours of the Divine Office.
Columban and all his monks were in the church, chanting
the psalms with the serenity and the minute attention to
every syllable, tone and genuflection which made their
prayer as of one body and one mind beyond the perturba-
tions of time. This was the monastery in its chief act of
worship next to the Mass, and for this the monks rose from
sleep, left cell or scriptorium, workshop or field, and pen-
alized themselves for unpunctuality or inadequate performance. It was a suitable hour for Count Bertechar and
his men to enter with the clash of feet and weapons, surround the church, and confront the abbot. There was a
spokesman, probably Bertechar.

"Man of God," it was said, "we beg you to obey both the
king's commands and ours, and leaving this place, to return by the same road by which you first came here."

This was the first part of the fate decided for Columban
by the boy, Theuderich, and the queen.

"I do not think," Columban replied, with a moving,
stark simplicity like that of one of the old Gaelic poems, "I
do not think it would please the Creator if a man were to
walk once again that native land he had left for the sake of
Christ."

It was more like a detached and deferential statement of
theology than a personal explanation. The detachment

made it all the harder to argue away. Count Bertechar saw the point. He ordered those soldiers who were known for their toughness to remain and carry out his orders; and then he rode away from the monastery. It seems that Count Baudulf also rode off, leaving the dirty business to the captain, Ragamund, and to his men.

The men who were supposed to be known for their determination in carrying out orders began to behave in a manner that would have horrified the more untamed Merovingians. They implored Columban to have pity on them. They were the unfortunate fellows that had been left behind to do the job. Let him consider the danger they were in; if they didn't take him away by force, their own lives would be in danger. He answered that he had often declared he would not depart except by violence. They realized they were in a fix, and from all sides they pleaded out of fear, crowding round him to pull at his habit, falling on their knees and begging with tears in their eyes that he should not blame them for this great crime because they were carrying out the king's commands and not their own wishes. He was a man of discipline who expected and demanded rigid obedience. He saw obedience now in the pleading soldiers, and he answered their pleas with the most difficult compassion of his life. From Luxeuil which he had founded on discipline he now decided to depart with that salute to discipline: compassion for men who would die if they failed in duty. He told his monks. It was the beginning of a long lamentation that was well remembered.

As he walked with his guards from the church, all his grieving monks formed behind him as if they followed in

his funeral procession. Apparently it was then that the pang
of separation hurt him, as if for the first time he felt the
knife that had been driven home in his flesh. He was being
separated from so many men who were a part of him as sons
are of a father. He stopped and prayed, and the prayer is
more like a cry: "O Eternal Creator, prepare a place for us
where we, Thy people, may serve Thee forever." He tried
to console these men who were like children, and he encouraged them not to lose hope but to continue to sing the
praises of Almighty God; what had happened to them was
not for their loss or his but for an increase of the number
of monks—and he spoke prophetically and with truth. He
then offered the monks a choice: whoever wished to follow
him should come with his mind made up fully to share
in sufferings; whoever wished to remain in the monastery
could do so with easy mind. Soon, God would avenge their
grief. No monk was willing to be separated from the abbot.

The guards had their orders. None would be permitted,
they informed the monks, to accompany Columban except
those from his own country or who had followed him from
Brittany; and the natives of Gaul must remain. The knife
turned again in the wound. Columban's grief became
sharper. He prayed once more for protection for those who
were being left behind, and around him there gathered,
hurrying with bundles and satchels for the journey, those
Irishmen and Bretons who had survived: Lua, Potentinus,
probably Aidus, Cominius, Eunoc, Equonanus, and most
certainly, Gall. The final farewell was given by a Burgundian of noble birth who had been a soldier: Eustasius,
disciple and minister to the abbot, who would, one day,

be himself abbot of Luxeuil. He clung to Columban, and he had to be dragged away by force like a child.

It was the twentieth year of Columban's sojourn in the desolation.

2

The intended, ultimate destination of the journey on which the captain, Ragamund, was ordered to escort Columban and the monks was Nantes. There, a ship was to be found that might rid the kingdom of these foreign trouble-makers.

It was probably in the spring or early summer that the party began the long, partly indirect march and river voyage that would cover over six hundred miles. They came down river valley after valley, from the Ognon to the Doubs, the Doubs to the Saône, keeping to the old roads that the Romans had maintained, and that were now, like the aqueducts and city paving and city walls, opening fissures and growing weeds in Merovingian neglect and war. It is likely that they passed through one of the towns in which Theuderich held court, Chalon on the Saône, before striking across through the vineyard slopes to Augustidunum (Autun). Every morning the mountains they had left were lower before the sun. There was haste. For the older men, for Columban himself who was seventy, there must have been increasing hardship and fatigue as the burden of the days of marching told on their strength. The prisoners, for such they were, had to find their own food, and in the kingdom of an infuriated king and under the watchful eyes of the escort there were some unprepared to succour the king's enemies.

From Autun, the route took a northerly direction along the ancient *via* to what was once a busy Roman station at Sidoloucum, now Saulieu, and thence to Avallon. The purpose of this journey along the Roman road which brought them northward to Autesiodorum, now Auxerre, and thence southward along another road to Nevers and to the river Loire, is obscure. Jonas provides tantalizingly meagre details of the whole journey, but of this return in direction he gives no details at all. At least two commentators propose a possible explanation as to why the party turned southward at Auxerre. The farther north the party advanced, they say, the deeper they went into territory which had been but lately wrested after a bloody battle by Theuderich's army from Clothair of Neustria; and the population being still unsubdued, there was greater danger of Ragamund and his escort being set upon. But then, why did they not strike westward from Auxerre to hit the Loire at least fifty miles north of Nevers and so save a journey of perhaps two days? It is possible that here, as at Autun or Avallon, they feared a journey across the forested hills, especially across the high cattle-country of the Morvan where the slant-eyed men of the region, said to have been descendants of Attila's hordes, were fiercely independent. Yet, they had no need to enter the Morvan for savagery.

As they came along the road near Avallon, a master of the king's horse rushed in a murderous rage, lance at the ready, to transfix Columban. He was, it is probable, a christened man in whom this terrible wrath blinded him for the moment to the meaning of the sacrilegious murder he was ready to commit. This monk was his king's enemy; this monk had made trouble in the kingdom: kill. He raised the lance; his arm went dead; the lance dropped and stood fixed in the ground, and he fell in convulsions at the feet of Columban. He had nearly accomplished the one thing that the king desired least of all, that is, to make a martyr of the Irish monk. Ragamund, the captain, must have been shaken. It appears that he even allowed the journey to be broken, for Jonas records that Columban kept the stricken, convulsed man close to him all that day and night, and that the next morning when light was breaking, he had him brought to him and cured him and the man returned to his home. Jonas had no doubt that a devil had been exorcised. Nor, one may surmise, had the captain and the soldiers any doubt.

Indeed, the whole journey is curiously marked off by cases of diabolic possession—or, at any rate, by cases of profound and violent nervous disorders—which Columban cured with the swift efficacy of a thaumaturge. Beyond Avallon, just at the Cure river before it enters the Yonne, they reached the house of a pious noblewoman named Theudemanda, and there he cured twelve demoniacs who rolled in convulsions of fury on the ground. It must have become more and more difficult for the captain, Ragamund, as this march of prisoners was met by more and more people. Hearing the news about the great abbot, they brought their sick and afflicted for his healing prayer and hand. The journey into ignominy was becoming uncomfortably like a triumphal procession. A few miles from Theudemanda's house, they entered the little town of Cure, near the modern Domecy-sur-Cure, and here five violently insane men were brought to him, and these, too, he quickly healed. In territory newly acquired in the bloody Merovingian way by King Theuderich, it looked unsafe for any king's man who might maltreat the wonder-worker. But Ragamund boasted of his king and his victory over King Clothair of Neustria. It evoked from Columban a political forecast about the kings which he was to repeat in various forms on subsequent occasions, each time using the term of three years as the date of the events he foretold. It was accurate. In the madly unsettled and unpredictable world of the Merovingians, it was a prediction sufficiently unexpected as to be reckoned prophetic.

"Remember, Ragamund," Columban said, "that Clothair, whom you now despise, will be lord within three years."

"Why, sir, do you say that?" Ragamund asked.

"What I say you will see happening, if you live till then."

This was at Auxerre, and it was remembered. They were then near the frontier of Neustria. As they were leaving the city, marching the descending road southward from one of the city gates, a young man who had run a great distance in a frenzy of madness came rushing towards them and collapsed at Columban's feet. It was another of the many halts while the abbot prayed and healed. Then the march went on, with the guards going before and behind, probably trying to keep up a pace that daily became more exhausting for the older men. The mountains they had left were to be seen no more, morning or evening. It was hilly country, heavily wooded, possessed by silence, until at last they began the descent into this valley of the upper Loire and saw the city of Nevers on its hill above the long

gleaming stretch of water that was to be their highway to
the sea. The monks were urged on. A boat was found, some
sort of skiff that moved probably by sail as well as by oars.
Even in a river-town like Nevers where traffic in timber,
wines, hides, grain and wool, as well as in people, had
made the citizens accustomed to the sight of strangers, the
monks must have looked strange: emaciated men, hollow-
cheeked, with shaven foreheads and long hair behind, dusty
from the march of nearly two hundred miles, and very
weary. Weariness had slowed them down. Impatiently, one
of the guards watched them stepping aboard the boat. He
picked up an oar and swung it and struck the monk Lua.
There was an outburst from Columban: "You cruel man,"
he cried out, "why do you add sorrow to sorrow? Hasn't the
evil you've done brought you enough guilt for your down-
fall? Why do you beat Christ's weary brothers? Why are
you harsh to the meek? Must you show savagery to the
gentle? Remember that in this very place in which you
struck one of Christ's brothers in your rage, you will be
struck by the vengeance of Heaven." Somebody heard the
outburst, remembered the soldier and the place, so that
Jonas could record it all and, in one of his less edifying
passages, tell how on the return journey the soldier was
drowned.

They slipped down the river on those peaceful waters
that must have been, even then, one of the serene glories
of Gaul. With cramped limbs in the confined space on the
boat, they could at least rest, pray, keep the Hours as
best they could, patch worn and broken sandals and repair
clothes, and watch the landscape slipping past beyond the
white islands of sand and the dense willows, the villages

beyond the limits of the winter floods, and the immobile eternal fishermen of the Loire. It is probable they had a pilot who was familiar with the current that threaded its way, more and more exiguously as the drier season advanced, between the islands and sand-spits. At any rate, they made good progress because their next stop was the city of Orleans, Aurelianum of the Roman conquest, now the nominal capital of the kingdom of Burgundy.

The king's orders had reached the city before the monks. They were harsh orders that had probably been formulated in anger against the reception given to Columban in some places on the road between Autun and Auxerre. All the churches in Orleans were closed against them; not only the churches but the lodging houses, so that they had to rest in tents on the banks of the river. There was worse to come.

Whatever supplies of food they had picked up on the road to Nevers were running out. They sent two monks into the city for food, and one of them, Potentinus, probably a Breton, was still living in a monastery in Coutances which he founded, when Jonas wrote. It was a day Potentinus could not forget. They crossed the city, questing for food, but they got nothing in shop or market or house. Fear of the king was in every citizen's heart. As they were returning with empty satchels down to the river by the same street as they had entered, they met a woman who stopped them. She was a foreigner like themselves, and something in their appearance, their robes and their tonsure must have stirred memories of the monks of the Syria from which she had come. She asked them who they were. They told her they had been questing for food and could get none.

"Come, my masters," she said, "to your servant's farm-house and take with you what you need. I also am a stranger here, from the far-off East."

They followed her gladly to her house and sat there on a stool, waiting until she brought what they were to take away with them. There was a man sitting with them, and he was quite still with the meekness of the blind. They asked her who he was.

"My husband," she answered, "also of the Syrian race. I lead him about because he lost the sight of his eyes many years ago."

They tell her that if she leads him to Christ's servant, Columban, perhaps his prayers will restore the blind man's eyes. Her husband has heard all this, and suddenly he is filled with faith, and be gets up to be led by her behind the two monks to Columban. They walk down to the tents on the river bank, and Potentinus tells Columban about how hospitably the Syrian woman has treated them in this city of closed doors and terrified people. The blind man immediately begs Columban to pray that he may see again. Columban turns to his monks and asks all of them to pray; he himself lies prostrate in prayer on the ground for a long time. At last he rises, makes the sign of the Cross on the man's dead eyes, and the man sees. He sees the abbot, the monks, his wife, the tents and the glittering sand and sparkling water and the stretching sky, with the joy that children and painters and poets sometimes experience.

In joy he went home, and probably in joy, he told the news. So, as before, the afflicted were brought to Columban, the diabolically possessed, for restoration to health. Se-cretly, the cowed citizens began to honour and help him, but they still feared the guards and the king's anger.

3

The captain, Ragamund, had need for greater care. No more delays at cities; no more time for yet another meeting of monk and people as at Orleans. The prisoners were herded on board the boat, and they pushed off into the widening shallow river for another stage in the long and drowsy journey. It was a good seventy miles from Orleans to Tours, through the loveliest of the Loire country, where among the vineyards and the long gentle hills kings and nobles of a later France would study pleasure as these men in the boat had studied penance. One place the monks knew about well, and it was Tours, Urbs Turonum on the south bank of the river. It meant little to them that it had been the capital of a Roman province and was a great city where bishop and saint, rather than king or count, had preserved even the secular virtues and much of Roman urbanity and civilization. For them, it was a holy place like Rome. It was the city of St. Martin.

They must have watched for it from far away on the river with more than the natural eagerness of pilgrims. Their devotion was native, brought with them from Ireland, where few saints were held in as high esteem. Martin the monk who had been a reluctant Roman soldier because he preferred Christian peace to war; Martin the reluctant bishop who had preached to the pagans of Gaul and blessed the land with miracles; Martin the pioneer of the monastic way of life: he was all these things among the Irish, and already he was being intensely commemorated, as he would be for century after century, and then transformed into a powerful wonderworking and weird figure of folklore in whose honour the mills would cease to grind on his feast-day, and the blood of a cock be sprinkled on the four corners of the house to bring a year's good fortune. But before that metamorphosis, there was the living power of the saint to whose tomb in a basilica in Tours the sick and the afflicted came for consolation if not for cure, and with them queens, and noble Gallo-Romans and Frankish lords, to pray among the silver lamps and the densely arrayed candles. The city was the dead man's city as surely as if he, an exile from Pannonia, had set out to conquer it. Where men prayed, Columban wished also to pray.

By this time the boat had slipped out of Burgundian territory into what was an Austrasian enclave. Tours belonged to Theuderich's brother, King Theudebert. The captain, Ragamund, whose instructions were to bring his prisoners to the sea at Nantes, most certainly dared not risk allowing them to land where he and his guards would be among potential enemies. Columban asked for permission to visit the tomb of St. Martin. Ragamund's reply was to urge the oarsmen to row quickly past the houses and the river wall and to order the helmsman to hold his course in the centre of the river. When Columban heard these commands, he began to pray sadly, complaining that he was not even permitted to visit the tombs of the saints. The oarsmen were pulling with all their strength, but as the boat arrived out in the river opposite the wharf its speed was checked as if it were being held by anchors, and it swung in towards the shore. Whether it was cross-current or miracle, the result was the same, and the oarsmen could do nothing except to let the boat take its own course. And as if it had wings, it floated from midstream to landing place. Columban was permitted to go where he pleased.

He went straight to the tomb of St. Martin, an exile, monk and missionary like himself, and there he spent the whole night in prayer. In the terms of his living, it was the first comfort he had had since the violent day many miles away in Luxeuil that the king's men entered the monastery church and prepared him for banishment. He had need of the comfort, need of the interior quietness in which he found strength to endure the anguish that was filling him for the sake of the abandoned monasteries. Would the monks, his people, remain a *muintir,* a *plebs,* a people undivided by the pressure that bishops and king could exert upon them? Would they, among themselves, remain undivided about the celebration of Easter and other things that the bishops had objected to? He had deep trust in that Burgundian noble-turned-monk, Attala, who was now father to the community in Luxeuil, but he felt that without his, Columban's, presence they might stand less firmly together. He had sweated under the burden of monastic government, trying to keep unity of the spirit in the bond of peace, bringing men's minds and hearts together in a day-long prayer compounded of the ordained practices of the liturgy and work and hunger and study. In bearing so much of the burden he had not been so wise, and he had almost been driven mad. Attala could be wiser. But the thought of him and of the monks could bring tears. A man had need of God's comfort and could find it beside the tomb of Martin.

News of Columban and his monks must have travelled through the city. At daybreak he was invited to the table of the bishop of Tours, Leuparius, and for the sake of the rest from travel the monks might receive, he accepted. That day, he remained with the bishop, and while he was seated at table with other guests the bishop asked him why he was returning to his native land. The old fiery temper flashed out as he said:

"That dog, Theuderich, has driven me from my brethren."

One of the guests, a man called Chrodoaldus, who was married to an aunt of the two royal brothers and was himself a follower of Theuderich, quoted a proverb in a low, conciliatory tone:

"It is better to drink milk than wormwood."

What he meant was, it seems, that King Theuderich had been lenient in not giving Columban worse treatment than banishment.

"I see," said Columban, "that you wish to keep your oath of loyalty to King Theuderich."

Chrodoaldus replied that he would keep his oath as long as he could.

"If," Columban retorted, "you are bound by an oath of loyalty to Theuderich, you will be glad to act for me as messenger to your friend and lord. Tell him," he added, repeating a prophecy already made to Ragamund the captain, "tell him that within three years he and his children will be destroyed and that his whole race will be uprooted."

"Why, man of God, do you say such things?"

"I cannot be silent about what God gives me to speak."

After that, there is silence in Jonas as if a hush had fallen on the dinner table of Bishop Leuparius; as indeed it might have fallen before that prophecy of the fall of a king and his whole house.

Columban returned to the boat and found his monks all depressed by the discovery of a great loss. On the previous night while they had been in the city, thieves had come and taken all they had, even the money that remained after they had given alms to the poor. What Columban did is childlike and slightly comic. He hurried to the basilica and upbraided St. Martin for allowing his friends to be robbed while they were visiting his tomb. Jonas gives no hint of what was said, but one may guess that it was not brief. For Jonas, it sufficed that the reproaches were effectual. One thief, groaning with pain, confessed where he had hidden the money, while his companions brought back what they had stolen and begged for forgiveness. It was enough for the thieves of the city who, thoroughly frightened, regarded as sacred all the monks' goods. From Bishop Leuparius Columban received all that he needed for the rest of the journey, the last stages down the river to Nantes.

There was a finality in these stages that Columban must have dreaded with a very human fear almost like a fear of death. Anybody in Tours would have told him how many leagues were yet to be travelled, but even if he had not inquired, he could have observed how the signs of finality grew more numerous. The river spread out wider and fuller from tributary waters until it was lake-like, dividing repeatedly round the elongated sandy islands where birds populated the osiers, willows and the tangled brush and driftwood of the winter floods. Men stood small in the distant fields that sloped up the sides of the wide valley. It was no desolation. The traffic of barges and rafts, boats and ferries, was more frequent, a sign of the great port and city ahead. Soon there were signs of what lay leagues beyond the city, out beyond the vast salt marshes blowing with reeds and coarse grasses. There were seabirds drifting in, the marks of tides on sleek mossy walls, and the smell of the sea on the west wind. Bird or tidemark or sea odour was each a last syllable in the sentence of banishment that was intended to carry Columban out into the infinity of the ocean. In the evenings the light was blazing full in their eyes.

But before that voyage so like death there would be the wait for the ship. It proved to be a prolonged wait. Somewhere in the big commercial and administrative city Columban and his friends found lodgings, probably near the quays among the poor since they themselves were poor men. Ragamund and the soldiers departed, but not, apparently, until he had spoken with the bishop, Soffronius, and with Theudoald, a count who was the king's representative, and informed them of Columban's case. This is an inference from the later churlish conduct of Theudoald and Soffronius.

One day a poor man came begging to Columban's lodgings.

"Give him something to eat," Columban said to his minister or attendant.

"We have no bread, only a little meal."

"How much have you?"

The attendant said they had no more than a measure.

"Give him all you have," Columban ordered, "and keep nothing for tomorrow."

The meal was given and nothing kept. The poor man
was fed, but for three days the monks went hungry. How
many of them remembered the long hunger during the
first days in the ruined fort at Annegray more than twenty
years previously, that is, if they had not longer hungers to
remember? As Jonas said, they had in Nantes only the
grace of faith and hope to keep the strength in their
exhausted bodies. On the third day, there came a loud
knocking on the door of that quiet house of famished men,
and the porter asked who it was but did not, it seems, open
to see. The caller answered that he had been sent by a
woman named Procula to feed Columban and his friends,
and that the food would arrive the next day. They were to
have the vessels ready, the jars and bins for a hundred
measures of wine, two hundred measures of corn and one
hundred of malt. It was biblical abundance. Another
woman named Doda sent two hundred measures of corn
and one hundred measures of mixed grain, which un-
doubtedly meant that the hungry poor of the city flocked
like starlings to the doorway of the lodgings.

The monks were making an impression on a busy city
that was sophisticated in its experience of foreign travellers.
The bishop, Soffronius, who had not merely given nothing
but also refused to sell anything to the monks, began to be
ashamed of himself. Jonas does not tell what this feeling of
shame made him do. In any case it was not strong enough
to restrain him from getting rid of the monks. He and
Theudoald began to insist that Columban board a ship
bound for Ireland. They must have met him and spoken
to him. His reply was not forgotten, a curious reply in

which he shows his desire to delay leaving Gaul as long as possible.

"If there is a ship sailing for Ireland," he said, "let all my companions and the baggage be put on board. I will take a small boat from the Loire as far as the open sea."

4

This was the event he had dreaded since they first told him in Luxeuil that he would be consigned back to his own country. It was termination: a ship, a voyage, Ireland, a man going back on the pilgrim road of utter exile that he had taken for Christ's sake. Anxiety for the monasteries and the monks had never left him. It now became an intolerable anguish of love, and sitting down in his lodgings, moved more deeply than perhaps be believed possible, he took pen and ink and parchment to write a farewell letter, words to send along the hundreds of miles of river highway and Roman road and country track. Such words as he wrote sprang from the intense affective emotions that annihilate space between soul and soul, as now they have the power to annihilate the centuries between us and that day of dereliction in Nantes. His humanity was never more amiable. He wrote:

"To his most sweet sons and dearest pupils, to his brothers in abstinence, to all his monks, Columban the sinner sends greeting in Christ.

"Peace be to you, as the Lord wished when He spoke to his disciples, and salvation and everlasting charity. These three things may the Trinity grant you through Him, and

keep them among you with my prayer. God alone Who
gave it knows the greatness of my zeal for your salvation
and how I long for your advancement in instruction; but
since in accordance with the Lord's teaching 'tribulation
and persecution because of the word' have arisen, no other
admonition is now fitting for you except that you take
care lest you be that stony ground which cannot nourish
the seed it receives in its poor soil. . . ."

The old anxieties are troubling him as he writes. It is
the fortitude of his monks he fears for, their patience in
manifold adversity; and he reminds them that it is not men
only who persecute them but men in whom there are
devils, envying the monks' spiritual possessions.

"Against them put on the armour of God to which the
apostle points and clear a path to heaven by shooting the
arrows, as it were, of your ardent prayers. Whatever you ask
for with faith and concord shall be given to you; but see
to it that you be of 'one heart and one soul' so that you
may get as a present reward whatever saving grace you
seek from the Father of Our Lord Jesus Christ, the common Father of us all . . . Otherwise if you do not possess
the same desire in the things you accept and reject, it is
better you do not live under the same roof. Therefore, I
charge all of you who agree with me in their hearts, and
who know and love my judgment, to remain with my true
follower, Attala, and let it be for him to choose to stay there
or to come after me; for he senses the danger to your
souls; do you obey him. If he should prefer to come to
me—and with God's help he will soon reach a definite
decision—let Waldelenus be the *praepositus*. Meanwhile,
take care lest there be any among you who does not be of

the same mind as you, whoever he may be; for we have
been harmed more by those among us who were not of one
mind with us."

What he remembers are painful things: disagreement
and discord. The monastic island set in the kingdom of
Burgundy had not been safely immune, and in his own
monastery among his own brethren he had found men
arguing for or supporting the bishops. He must have
trusted them and then found minds that did not think like
his. The burden of controversy with the bishops had become a domestic grief. And now there was Attala on whose
shoulders all the burdens were being placed. So, his letter
turns to his faithful follower:

"You know, dearest Attala, those who are troublesome
to you. Dismiss them at once, but dismiss them in peace
and according to the Rule; only be sure to honour
Libranus, and always keep Waldelenus; if he is there with
the community, may God be good to him, may he be
humble, and give him my kiss which then in the hurry he
did not receive.

"You have, indeed, long known my purpose of develop-
ing abilities; if you see some souls progressing, stay there;
if you see dangers, come here; but the dangers I mean are
the dangers of discord, for I fear that there, too, there may
be discord about Easter . . . now without me you seem to
stand less firmly . . . be wiser than I have been; for I would
not have you take up the burden under which I have
sweated . . . therefore be many-sided and adaptable in the
care of those who obey you with faith and love, but you
must fear their love itself lest it become dangerous to you.
. . . But there is danger if they hate and danger if they

love. Know that both are real, be it their love or hatred;
peace perishes in hatred, and integrity in love. Hold yourself then to the force of the one desire which you know
my own heart desires. . . ."

The one desire was the perfection of each one of the
brethren according to the Rule. His thoughts come in less
and less logical order. What he writes has the pathos of a
man who wishes to speak to his dearest friends and has too
much to say and too little time to say it. He had wanted to
write a grieving letter, but preferring to restrain rather
than encourage tears, he mentions duties. Yet, tears flow.
They are the tears of intense suffering. But suffering is not
new. Christ willingly mounted the cross as a criminal,
and blessed is the man who becomes a sharer in this Passion
and this shame. Meditating on the mystery of the Passion,
he lets his pen fly on. Across those hundreds of miles he
preaches a sermon to his brethren about the meaning of
salvation, the weakness of men and the mercy of God. And
as he writes, the knock comes on the door of his lodgings,
and a messenger is there to say that the ship is waiting,
ready to bear him unwilling to his own country. He can
add only a little more. Quickly, he writes that if he escapes,
there is now no guard to prevent him. Indeed, it seems to
him that they wish him to escape.

"If," he writes with gentle humour, punning in the old
fashion on his name, "if I am cast into the sea like Jonah,
who himself is also called dove in Hebrew, pray that someone instead of a whale may, in safe concealment by a happy
voyage, bring your Jonah back to the land he longs for.
But now my parchment letter is forced to an end . . . love
does not keep order, and so my missive is confused. . . ."

And with a dozen or more lines of rapid counsel, he at last writes the final prayer, "Pray for me, *viscera mea*, that I may live to God." How can one translate *viscera mea*? His monks are the beloved of his soul, the very depths of his being.

His companions in Nantes were ready. What baggage they possessed must have been scanty, for they were travelling men with little love for gear or goods. A cargo ship trading with Ireland had been found at last, and his monks went on board with all their belongings. The vessel worked its way, with oars and sail, down the long channel that led towards the open Atlantic while he, as he had promised, remained behind to take a small boat and presently follow them. Out of the sky came salvation. While he was still waiting, a storm blew up, tearing up the channel across the marshes and the mudflats, and the ship, caught between river and wind, was driven high and dry on the shore. For three days that wind blew with the ship aground. Whatever it was that the captain believed—and sailors find strange beliefs in their traffic with the sea—he decided that his misfortunes were because of the monks and their belongings, and he unloaded everything that belonged to them, and got them ashore. With the next tide, the ship floated.

This was the escape for Jonah. It was now taken as clear that God did not wish him and his monks to return to Ireland. They went back to their lodgings, free men, on whom the citizens lavished respect and assistance. Nantes was to hold them, however, only for a short while more.

5

Suddenly, Jonas the biographer has Columban on the road once more.

The journey cuts northeastward across Gaul through the extended kingdom of Austrasia and into the diminished kingdom of Neustria. As a sustained march for veteran soldiers, well-fed and travelling light, those hundreds of miles would have been a minor feat, but for some of the old monks who had lived all their lives on meagre rations, short sleep and hard work, the march was something soldiers might envy. Jonas gives not one detail of that march. At the end of one paragraph, Columban is in Nantes; almost at the beginning of the next, he is in Soissons, at the court of King Clothair, son of the terrible Fredegund. One gets a definite impression of speed and secrecy. These are men who have escaped; they are determined not to suffer the Burgundian enmity again; indeed, their decision seems to be to leave tormented, riven Gaul in which Merovingian kings, their mayors and nobles, have been planning and waging wars, making and remaking frontiers, and working as if they obeyed some doom, towards annihilation.

It was enough for King Clothair that Columban had suffered at the hands of Theuderich, his cousin, and of Brunhilde, his own mother's enemy. He welcomed the exiled abbot and the monks, offered him land in his territories and promised help in every way. Columban refused, saying that he did not wish to settle down in that region;

and his biographer, Jonas, is not sure why he refused. In fact he attributes a choice of two reasons to Columban: either that he wished to continue his wanderings as a pilgrim or that he wished to avoid all danger of further hostility. But the two reasons are valid. For the rest of his life, Columban would not remain for long in any place, and his journeys would take him farther along that road, generally southward, across the mountains into Italy and towards that Rome which he had wished to visit. Besides, Gaul was uneasy with rumours of war.

Clothair kept him as long as he could be persuaded to stay. A rest was needed in any case, as well as time to prepare for another journey. Columban in return gave the king the gift that the Merovingians so often refused, to their cost: he castigated him for some of the usual follies of the royal courts, and the king promised amendment. He seems to have liked Clothair, who reaches the pages of Jonas as a man of sound wisdom.

Clothair was at least cunning. In his diminished kingdom which had already lost territories and cities to the attacks of his two cousins, Theudebert and Theuderich, he bided his time, knowing in his very blood that those two brothers would yet wage war on each other. While Columban was with him, the dispute about frontiers was boiling up between the brothers. Both sent agents to Clothair, asking for his aid. Out of genuine respect for his shrewdness, or out of a superstitious awe of him as a prophet, Clothair asked Columban for advice.

"Take sides with neither," Columban answered. "Within three years, both kingdoms will be yours."

It was the third occasion on which he had set the term

of three years to the power of Austrasia and Burgundy.
Clothair did not follow the advice to the letter. He accepted a treaty with Theuderich, while at the same time
he promised Theudebert aid in case of attack.

It was no air for monks to breathe. This was not their
world. They prepared to depart towards the Alps and
Italy. As their direction would take them through the
territory of King Theudebert, Columban asked Clothair
for an escort, and this he was given. For some unexplained
reason, they turned southwest towards Paris, and at a
gate of that city, a noisy and violent country town crowded
against the wide bend of the Seine, there occurred another
encounter with a demoniac.

While Columban is still some distance away marching
with the escort, this poor writhing creature shouts in a
croaking, complaining voice:

"What are you doing here, man of God?"

Columban reaches him, looks, and says:

"Depart, you evil one. Depart and do not dare again to
enter the bodies that have been washed in Christ's Baptism. Yield to God's power, and tremble at the spoken
name of Christ."

But as the man continues to struggle with a savage and
malevolent strength, Columban stretches out his hand, puts
it into the slavering mouth and draws out the tongue, while
again commanding the unclean spirit to depart in the name
of God. Now the man struggles and twists with a strength
that can break bonds, and his bowels heave, and he vomits
and befouls himself. A fetor, more sickening than the
stench of sulphur, strikes the nostrils of the bystanders.
Then the man is very quiet, cured.

All this at a gate of Paris. It is a scene too harsh and brutally grotesque for the fine hands that carved the Frankish ivories. This is surely for carven stone, high on the façade of one of the cathedrals of a later age, even for the high gothic of Notre-Dame that would one day rise on the island in the Seine: a saint in stiffly draped robes bending towards a man with the wide staring eyes and open fanged mouth of the half-devil.

To where Notre-Dame now stands, Columban may have gone, indeed surely did go, to pray in the basilica of St. Stephen. A Merovingian king, Childebert, had built it, and one must look at it, even for a moment, not merely because Columban may have prayed there but because it represents the strong, impulsive religious nature of those strange kings. It is one of the glories of the crowded town where the beautifully cut Roman stone of temples, arches and villas are now used for barns, houses, fortresses, gates, sarcophagi and abbeys. All the past is muddled and mingled, Roman, Gaul and Frank, with the new violent present, and in the narrow streets the monks rub elbows with Clothair's soldiers wearing skins and furs and jewelled buckles, merchant Jews, Syrians and Egyptians selling spices, embroidered textiles, perfumes, gems, and geegaws. For all of them, the basilica is a wonder of the West, to be compared with Solomon's temple. It is simple in structure, about one hundred and fifty feet by seventy, with walls two feet thick in some places, the lower courses being of Roman masonry. The surface texture is brilliant with tile, glass, brick, stucco and variegated stone embedded in showy designs in the masonry. There are swastikas and spirals, six-petalled roses, triangles and hexagons. Inside, the walls, the floors and the ceilings are alive with colours, with iridescent frescoes, with geometric figures unlooping themselves in the mosaics of the floor, and with golden mosaics in the apse. The colours, the gold, and the jet-black pillars reflect the flames of hundreds of lamps and candles.

It was still not Columban's world. It was a church in a city. By tradition and experience and by the nature of the monastic life, he and his monks did not belong to cities. If he had to live for long in any secular place in Gaul, his choice would certainly have been one of the villas on one of the self-contained farming estates in which life was cut off from the world's traffic and followed the routine and rhythm of the seasons.

It was towards such a great house that he now moved eastwards from Paris along the valley of the Marne. This house stood a few miles from the city of Meaux and was called **Pipimisiacum**. The house and the vast estates attached to it had once been within the fluctuating Burgundian frontier, but now it stood in Austrasia, the kingdom of Theudebert, and its owner, Chagneric, was one of the most powerful of Theudebert's courtiers.

Chagneric was no stranger to Columban. His house was a hospitable Christian place. His son, Chagnoald, had been a pupil and then a monk at Luxeuil for sixteen or seventeen years, and this was the monk who told Jonas about how the squirrels and other little creatures as well as the birds used to gambol and frisk with Columban in the wilderness. Chagneric and his wife, Leudegund, welcomed the wandering abbot and the monks and promised all the help necessary for reaching the court of King Theudebert at Metz. The escort was dismissed; there would

now be no need of it. Chagneric himself would make ar-
rangements for the safe journey. But he had another motive
as well: he wished to keep Columban as long as possible so
that his house might be blessed by his teaching, or rather,
that it might be ennobled by it. His house was blessed
and ennobled in a way he, a worldly man, never expected.
He had already given Chagnoald to religion, and for his
other children, two sons and two daughters, he probably
had the vague plans that any noble Frankish father settled
on early, possibly at the side of the cradle. The sons would
advance in the service of the king. The daughters would
be married off conveniently to powerful lords.

There must be a divine irony in an account of the effects
of Columban's visit. He blessed the house and he blessed
the children. Towards the youngest, Fare, a little girl of
seven or eight years, he showed a tenderness that makes
his monumental sternness most human. According to one
of the stories about her—and Jonas tells many in other
writings but oddly enough not this one!—when Columban was about to depart, he found to his astonishment
that she was playing with a head of wheat although the
time of harvest was not near. He read into it a sign of
things to come, and he said to her that she had chosen a
great happiness and that the wheat would be her portion
in life. The child did not understand. He explained
that this head of wheat was a symbol of Jesus Christ, who
had been cast on the earth like a wheat-grain, and beaten
and threshed like the harvest in His Passion; that He had
suffered and died so that men might be nourished and
might live eternally. They said other things to each other,
the child and the aged monk, and what he said was in

itself like the sowing of a grain of wheat that would grow up and multiply and become a field. This child of Chagneric's became, at first against her father's will, a hermit, and then the abbess and founder, under Columban's Rule, of one of the most famous monasteries of Gaul, *Farae monasterium,* Faremoutiers. Saxon kings would send their daughters there for schooling; and a daughter of Charlemagne would be abbess. Her brother Chagnoald would become bishop of Laon, and another brother, Faro, bishop of Meaux.

Where Columban went, he went like a sower. He continued his journey up the Marne, and hardly twelve miles from Chagneric's villa he was welcomed in another great house on the right bank of the confluent Grand-Morin. The place was called Vulciacus, now Ussy, and the owner, Autharius, welcomed the monks. Once again, divine irony sharpens the story. Autharius and his wife, Aiga, brought their three sons to be blessed by Columban, who was impressed by the mother's piety. The young boys were blessed, and Columban went on his way on the long road that would lead comparatively soon to death in Italy; and they grew up, Frankish men taking their places at the courts of kings. Then, one by one, they forsook the world. Ado, the eldest, became a monk, and under the Rule of Columban founded the double monastery of Joarre on a height above the confluence of the Marne and the Petit-Morin. Rado, the second son, treasurer of a Merovingian king, never became a monk, but he laid the foundations of the abbey of Reuil. The youngest, Dado, afterwards called Audoenus, renounced his life as king's counsellor and founded a monastery at Rebais in the depths of the forest of La Brie, and as first abbot he selected Agile, Columban's disciple and Chagnoald's cousin. It was as if an army had passed over this corner of Gaul and conquered it, unknown to the inhabitants.

CHAPTER 6

The High Mountains

1

WHAT was in fact a small army continued its march of some one hundred and sixty miles, across river valley after valley, to where King Theudebert held court in Metz. Messengers from Chagneric must have ridden for days before them both to the king and to the monastery at Luxeuil. Theudebert welcomed them most warmly. But there were others to give welcome, men Columban had never expected to see again and who, while he thought of them in Nantes, had drawn tears from his eyes. Here, come all the way from Luxeuil to join him, were Chagnoald, Attala, Eustasius, and many others. They would travel with him along a great part of this, his last interrupted journey towards Italy, and at different places some of them would, as it were, step aside to found a monastery and make the name of Columban remembered in yet another place, a mountain village or a lakeside town. The wheat that had been stored in the barns of Luxeuil would be given a fine scattering in the springtime of the new Europe. For Columban, these monks who had marched up the Roman road from Luxeuil were, to use Jonas's words, as booty recovered from the enemy!

Would there never be an end to the journeys? A wandering monastery is a community that can lose discipline, neglect the corporative routine despite itself and fall to pieces. Stability was an essential. King Theudebert, to whom Columban must have mentioned his anxieties in the matter, promised that he would assign to them a suitable place in his territory from which they could bring the faith to the neighbouring peoples. The thought of preaching to the heathen had been in Columban's mind for some time, certainly since the banishment. Here was an opportunity, among the peoples of Rhenish Austrasia.

"If," Columban said, who was wary of kings, "you keep your promise, I will stay in your kingdom for a while, and try to sow the faith in the hearts of the people."

"The king," says Jonas, "allowed them to select any place they wished." This meant that Columban had all of Austrasia as his field, as well as Alsace, which had been very recently ceded by Theuderich after his brother had made a show of force. Indeed, it is very likely that this dispute was the one about which Clothair of Neustria had asked Columban's advice. Jonas goes on to say that the monks chose Bregenz. Very quickly, with only a halt at Mainz where they meet with an adventure, he has them in the old ruined town of Bregenz, standing on its eminence, on the southeast shore of Lake Constance.

It was, of course, a journey of many weeks and of hundreds of miles, most of it by water. King Theudebert appears to have been regally generous. He provided them with boatmen and a boat which brought them down the

winding valley of the Moselle to Coblenz, the lovely valley
that Ausonius (a poet Columban knew and echoed) had
caught in verse like a little coloured world imprisoned
forever in glass: quiet waters, the evening star bringing
the evening shadows, the green slopes filling the river with
their reflections, the hilltops wavering under the ripples,
and the vineyards swaying in the clear crystal of the flood.
Such travel with the current of a peaceful river is a healer,
and for the monks who had marched as many hundreds
of miles it must have meant a renewal of vigour.

One day, as Jonas tells, they came to Mainz. The long
journey had taken toll of their supplies of food. One can
only surmise that while Theudebert had been generous
with boatmen and food, he had failed to give the monks
any money. At any rate, they were in need when they
reached Mainz. The boatmen said to Columban that
they had friends in the city who would give them all they
needed. Columban told them to go ahead. Presently they
returned and confessed that they had been unable to get
anything from their friends.

"Let me," said Columban, "go to see my friend for a
little while."

He left them wondering how he could have a friend in
a city he had never visited. Going to a church, he entered
and cast himself on the pavement on his knees and prayed
for a long time. Soon, the bishop of the city—his name was
Leonisius—happened to come from his palace to visit the
church, and seeing Columban, he asked him who he was.
Columban said he was a traveller, a *peregrinus*.

"If you need any food," the bishop answered, "come to
my house and take whatever you need."

Then the bishop sent his servants to the boat to tell the monks and the boatmen, with the exception of one left on guard, to come and take away what they wished. "Let no one," sternly warns Jonas, "think that all this happened by chance."

They were soon travelling up the broad Rhine. The ascent must have meant a tremendous sustained effort for the boatmen, what with rowing and towing when the wind was unfavourable to the use of sails. Jonas is silent about the arduous journey, silent about the cities and the halting places, Worms and Speyer and Seltz, and the voyage up the course of the Aare and Limmat into Lake Zürich. "In due time," he says simply, "they reached their destination."

The destination was near Bregenz, the territory of the Alamannians. One wishes that he had inquired about that river journey and told the story of it, but even if he had told it, the story would have been of his time and method: merely the names of places and a few curious details, as if travel when it was most arduous were just a task to be got through and done with. But to that journey belongs the rowing-song, the only Christian example of its kind, which has been attributed to Columban.

It consists of twenty-four hexameters, with a refrain which is repeated after every second line until, in the middle, it changes and invokes the name of Christ. "The long sweep of the rhythms," observes Walker, "gives to this poem a quality of untiring strength." Who chanted it, one wonders, on that voyage? It is not the folksong of unlettered boatmen in the service of a Frankish king but of a man learned in the classics, for he lifts two lines wholly, and three partly, from Virgil. And the refrain,—even the

basic pattern of the poem—was not his original idea. The
refrain and its variant run, with Walker's translation:

> *Heia viri! nostrum reboans echo sonet heia!* . . .
> Ho, my men! Let ringing echo sound our Ho! . . .
> *Vestra, viri, Christum memorans mens personet heia!*
> Let your mind, my men, recalling Christ sound Ho!

What had come into Columban's mind was an older,
pagan rowing-song, now of unknown date and authorship,
and with that happy unawareness of guilt in plagiary with
which the ancients were blessed, he used it and made it
his own:

En silvis caesa fluctu meat acta carina
Bicornis Hreni et pelagus perlabitur uncta.
Heia viri! nostrum reboans echo sonet heia!

This Walker translates:

Lo, cut in forests, the driven keel passes on the stream
Of twin-horned Rhine, and glides as if anointed on the flood.
Ho, my men! Let ringing echo sound our Ho!

2

The Alamannian territory to which they had come
singing among the mountains and across a lake that was
like a sea of glass was no country for faint-hearted preach-
ers. It had a beauty and a quiet majesty such as they had
never experienced on any of their journeys, and the light

from water and sky was like a liberation of the spirit. All round the lake men had lived for centuries, enduring raids and conquest, creating meadows and cornfields on the gentle lower lacustrine slopes, and vineyards and orchards on the upper where the forests began their ascending march to the skyline. In the distance the Alpine peaks shone with snow. It was almost a world set apart, but the Romans had come, threading a road up from Italy through valleys and passes, over the Septimerberg to the lake and the way into Gaul. At the head of the lake they had built a fortress, Turicum, Zürich, for subjugation of the peoples. By the time Columban and his monks arrived, the Roman peace had been long broken, the eagles were a memory, the town buildings were in ruins and on the highway the marsh grasses and the forest were moving in to erase what Roman skill had fashioned. Living in the valleys and on the lakeshore were the descendants of the people that the legions had failed to defeat.

For more than four centuries these, the Alamannians, had fought as part of a vast loose Germanic confederation that came out of the forests between the Rhine and the Danube. At first the Romans had barely held them, bought them off, and at last failed to stand. Defeats never chastened these warriors who returned again and again in increasing numbers like animals in migration, swarming along the river valleys, bursting into the fortified towns, engulfing the military stations, raiding Gaul and raiding even as far south over the mountains as Ravenna. Early in the fifth century, they crossed the Rhine in strength, conquered and settled in Alsace and a large part of Switzerland. But their dominion was brief. Where the legions had failed, another warlike people, the Franks, succeeded. The Alamannians met and for a while battled successfully with their Frankish enemies; but at last they went down in slaughter on the field of Tolbiac before the armies of Clovis, the founder of the Merovingian dynasty. This was the battle on which Clovis more or less gambled about renouncing his own gods and accepting Christianity. There was no one among the Alamannians to make such a gamble: defeated, they clung obstinately and grimly to their own language, customs and religion—as Columban and his monks were to learn. They were the only Germanic tribe that had resisted the influence of the Romans. Although they were in contact with the Christianized cities and with the Christian Franks who administered the royal estates and worshipped God in chapels dedicated to St. Martin or St. Hilary, they still held to the ancient pieties, venerated the gods of sky and earth, trees, rivers and mountains, and offered sacrifice of horses, oxen and other animals. A few became Christians. Many must have been conscious of how their Frankish overlords scorned their heathenism. But they would not yield for decades, and then only with reluctance. They were in their fashion a most faithful people.

For Columban's first real encounter with them we must turn, not to Jonas, but another biographer, Walafrid Strabo, the "Squinter," who in the ninth century wrote the life of St. Gall at the request of an abbot of the eponymous monastery that saint founded. He was a scholar of Reichenau and of Fulda, tutor of a prince who became king of Neustria, a poet of sorts and a lover of gardens. When he sat to write the life of Gall, he had the work of Jonas before

him. It is he who gives us the account of the monks' first
encounter as missionaries with the Alamannians on the
shores of Lake Zürich.

The monks had worked their way along the lake till they
reached the southern end. Here on the shore-lands around
the river Linth and in neighbouring valleys, the Alamannians had settled down, and their most populous settlement, Tuggen, today some two miles inland from the
receded waters, stood at the edge of the lake. Tuggen
looked like a suitable site for a monastery. The monks set
to work, building temporary shelters which were probably
no more than wattled huts, and began to preach.

Up to this time, Columban and his monks had never
encountered so pagan a people as the Alamannians who, as
Walafrid Strabo wrote, were savage image-worshippers
given to offering sacrifices to idols and to practising augury
and divination. We are not told what the idols were, nor
what the gods. It is fairly certain that Wodan, whom the
Romans identified with Mercury, and the other northern
deities such as Frigga his wife, Balter his son, and Mimir
his uncle were among them. But not even the Alamannians
could discern the metamorphoses those images of power
had endured during the prolonged racial migrations
through the forests, and how the attrition of the centuries
had altered the myth of Wodan, the frenzied one, source
of wisdom and valour, patron of heroes, war god and giver
of victories. Whatever the gods were, it is clear that they
were hateful to the monks, who apparently made no effort
to discover what truths, what aspirations, lay latent or
explicit in the Alammanian beliefs. Indeed, it is quite

clear that the monks went directly into conflict with belief
in the old gods. At least, one monk did.

He was Gall, the man who appears to have had a special
gift for learning foreign tongues. He had been Columban's
pupil and disciple in Bangor. In the life of the abbot as
related up to this time by Jonas, Gall is a monk muffled in
an almost seamless silence. When he is mentioned, he is
being chastised as a fisherman who cast his net in a river
other than the one indicated by Columban. Otherwise, he
is a shadow. One deduces the fact of his existence in the
Burgundian monasteries and on the journeys to and from
Nantes. He has the anonymity of a shadow. One can only
say that he is there, equally anonymous with his brethren
among that procession of figures trudging along the forest
rides and the roads, walking the narrow streets of Soissons
or Paris or Metz, or stepping from a boat on to the shore
of Lake Zürich near where it receives the Linth. He is
anonymous in obedience as a man might be in a soldier's
uniform, and only his skill as a fisherman and his ability
as a learner of languages can yet distinguish him from the
others. Then, unexpectedly, he comes forward with violence and a flaming torch.

The monks had begun teaching the Alamannians to
worship, as Walafrid Strabo says, the Father, the Son and
the Holy Ghost, and to keep the faith in its true form. But
they were dealing with an obstinate people who clung to
the gods they had brought with them. Then, full of zeal,
Gall set fire to the temples where sacrifices were made and
threw all the offerings he found into the lake. The reaction
of the Alammanians was, apparently, slow, but it cannot
have been a complete surprise to the monks. The Alaman-

nians became angry and hostile. As Walafrid Strabo wrote,
they began to persecute the brethren and formed a plan
to kill Gall, scourge and humiliate Columban and banish
them from their settlement. Among them there must have
been some friendly souls, because Columban was told
about the plot.

The news forced him to a drastic decision. The Alamannians had refused to hear; he and his monks would shake
the dust of Tuggen off their sandals and depart. What was
the use of wasting on this stiff-necked, ungrateful crew the
labour that might be of profit to men of good will? But, as
Strabo says, before he left he pronounced a curse upon
them which by its terrible violence—death and madness
for children, oppression of the people by tyrants—is
probably a reflex of the barbaric violence with which he
and his monks had been affronted.

The monks departed, and one may surmise that they
went quickly and secretly. Their route was generally in a
northeasterly direction through what had been Roman
villages and camps towards Lake Constance where, on the
southern shore, they found a Christian community in the
old Roman colony of Arbon. This was a world less rugged,
more suave and humanized. Deep woods covered the
green hills that sloped down to the pale green lake that
spread like a small sea. A day's easy ascending march
back in the hills, there was a high place in which it was
Gall's earthly destiny to do his life's work, and his days,
and leave his name. But that was all yet to come when
they walked into the little lakeside town of Arbon and met
a priest named Willimar. He was a good man.

When he saw Columban approaching, staff in hand,

with his laden monks, he cried out, "Blessed is he that comes in the name of the Lord."

"The Lord," Columban replied, "has gathered us out of the lands."

After the primitive harshness of the time spent at Tuggen, the Christian salutation comes new and joyful. The priest took Columban by the right hand and led him into his oratory, where they prayed together, presumably with the monks. There is in this act a ritual hospitality, as if Christians could not be strangers. Then, Willimar brought them to his house, and they laid down their baggage and rested. It was of Christian things they discoursed in that house, and Gall's voice is heard once more, breaking the silence that has surrounded him. What he talked about, whether it was some passage of Scripture, some aspect of the mysteries of God, the Trinity and man's redemption, we do not know; but Gall spoke with such wisdom that the priest Willimar wept. One guesses that in his welcome there was an expression of his loneliness and of his need, in the small isolated old Roman *castrum*, for the company of learned Christian men. For a week he kept the monks in his house, fed them, became their servant, and asked for no more than this company for which apparently he had hungered.

One day, Columban asked him if he knew of any place in an uninhabited district where they could build a *cellula*, a cloister, so that they might follow their monastic life. The very question betrays the permanent anxiety of the nomadic abbot who knows by experience the harm that wandering can do to a community. Willimar knew of a place not far away near the ruined buildings of a town; the soil was fertile; and there were high hills all around.

He told them the place was called Brigantium—the site of
the old town of Bregenz on the southeastern shore of Lake
Constance.

3

Ruins; wilderness; ground to till; isolation: it seemed
like a description of old Annegray or Luxeuil. Columban
was eager to go, and Willimar the priest, who was as eager
to help, found a boat for them and manned it with rowers
for the lake-voyage of fifteen or sixteen miles. Columban
took Gall with him, and as guide a deacon of Willimar's
whose name was probably Hiltibod. At least, it is Hiltibod
who figures in Walafrid's life of Gall as a man who was
familiar with every nook and cranny of the wilderness because he was a fisherman and a hunter.

They crossed to ruined Bregenz and landed near a place
where there stood an oratory in which Christian men had
worshipped and prayed before the flood of invading peoples had submerged Roman power and Roman civilization.
The oratory had been dedicated to St. Aurelia. She is a
dim, disputed figure among the hagiographers, hardly
more substantial than a name. Because she was also venerated at Rome and Anagni, it has been inferred that she
was an Italian, who probably died in the fourth century
near Strassburg where Columban and his monks may have
prayed in an ancient church dedicated to her and received
a gift of some of her relics. Whatever they had learned of
her in Strassburg, Arbon or Bregenz, they knew her oratory
had been a place of Christian worship before Wodan's

people had come and defiled it. They knelt and prayed and
then set about surveying the neighbourhood.

It is curious that Jonas says the place did not please the
monks and that Walafrid contradicts him. According to
Walafrid they were very pleased with both the situation
and the aspect. Jonas may have been recording memories
of later unpleasantness among the Alamannians and Walafrid may have been referring solely to the physical ameni-
ties, to the fertile soil, the isolation, the suitability of the
location as a mission centre, and the immense sweeping
prospect that embraced almost the entire lake stretching
westward as far as a man could see: the pine-wooded high
crags to the east; to the south the green valley of the upper
Rhine; and against the sky the Alpine peaks cloud-high and
ghostly with snow.

The rest of the monks were brought from Arbon to
begin work on the new monastery that was to stand on the
ground given by that now remote king, Theudebert of
Austrasia. He had probably never ridden or seen this land
of his and never would, and he never could possess it as
the monks set about possessing it with axe and spade. They
cleared the spaces of brushwood and trees for gardens and
fields, and built their little cells, and under the suspicious
slow regard of the barbarians turned to restore the oratory
of St. Aurelia. In the oratory they found affixed to a wall
two or three images of gilt bronze which the Alamannians
worshipped. What were they? "These," the people said,
"are the old gods, and it is by their help that we and ours
have been kept and nourished up to this day." They
honoured these old gods on certain days by gathering in
festival and offering them gifts and making sacrifices.

It was then just the time for a gathering, and a great crowd of men and women had come in from the farms round about and from the hills, not only to celebrate the festival but to see these strangers, weather-beaten travellers from a distant world who spoke strange tongues, worked from dark to dark, moved with a measured, controlled quietness, and frequently made on themselves, on the axes they cut with and the spades they dug with, and on the doorways they entered, that simple sign of the Christians. But one man could speak to them in words they could understand. He was Gall, on whom Columban had laid the duty of preaching.

It is precisely in Gall and through Gall since "he had no small knowledge of the barbaric idiom," as Walafrid wrote, that one world met and spoke to another; the world of Christ and the Apostles, Rome and the martyrs, of the monks in Egypt and Syria and Ireland on the edge of the northern ocean, speaking to a people who had come with the wrath of war out of the continental forests: the Word-Made-Flesh answering the dark riddles and the violent gropings of the mythologies. Gall waited till the crowd had gathered around the oratory where the monks prayed, and then in obedience to the abbot's command, he began to tell them the truth of Christ and to exhort them to turn from the worship of images, the shapes of gilt bronze that stood against the wall. He then went and took down these images, broke them with stone, carried the pieces down to the lakeside and threw them into the waters. He must have been fairly sure that his dramatic actions would not provoke the people to vindictive violence, as had happened at Tuggen, and that he would find some among them who were prepared to listen. Some did, indeed, listen, and these were the first converts, but others who revered the old gods went away full of rage and resentment. That day was not yet finished. The gods were broken, but the oratory had to be repossessed. Columban ordered water to be brought, blessed it, sprinkled the building and dedicated it anew while the monks walked in procession around it, chanting psalms. He went to the altar, washed it, probably with wine and water, anointed it with blessed oil, placed within it the relics of St. Aurelia, laid upon it an altar-cloth and then celebrated Mass.

There are few pages in Jonas as vivid as Walafrid's description of that day when Gall preached and broke the images, and Columban ritually cleansed the oratory and said Mass. The drama of the day was of the kind that might easily have passed into folklore and certainly into the lore of the monasteries which Columban's monks founded or inhabited in Switzerland. But it was only a beginning, an initial gesture that could impress. It would merely preface the months, the years of hard work, preaching, teaching, ministering, building and tilling, all within the monastic routine. Columban and "his fellow-soldiers," as Walafrid calls the monks, stayed in the place for about two years. They built a small cloistered monastery, laid out a garden and cultivated fruit trees, while Gall, the indefatigable fisherman, wove nets and fished the lake so that there was always abundance for the brethren and for the passing travellers. Columban, very likely with Gall as interpreter and companion, went about among the people, and on one of those exploratory journeys he had an adventure which in the pages of Jonas reads more like a passage from a folktale than from hagiography.

The oratory of St. Aurelia had been rededicated, but in the forests, in the pagan settlements, the old gods were still being worshipped. On one occasion he came upon an assembly grouped round a large vat, capable of holding twenty measures, full of beer. It was not a tribal drinking party, as he discovered when he approached and put questions. They told him that they intended to offer the vat of beer to Wodan. Did the vat bear some mystical relation to the magic cauldron of the northern mythology? It made no difference to the old man whether it did or not. He went to the vat, breathed on it, and it burst with a loud noise so that all the beer flowed out on the ground. This is the story that Jonas told soberly, but one hopes that he smiled when he added that the astounded barbarians declared that the man of God had great strength in his breath! Columban then preached to them and told them to return to their homes, and while some were convinced of the truth of what he uttered, others, no doubt, resented his interference.

In a most eerie passage which is capable of interpretation without recourse to howling demons, Walafrid tells a story that illustrates the agonized dying of the old pagan religion. Once upon a time, Gall was out fishing on the lake casting his nets in the silence of the night. He heard a voice—Walafrid says it was a demon's—calling loudly from the summit of a nearby mountain and being answered by another voice from the lake. Voice called to voice, complaining about the strangers who had come from afar, taken over the temple, shattered the images, and

drawn after them the people who used to follow the old
gods. On hearing the voices, Gall "made himself safe on
every side with the sign of the holy cross," and cried out:
"In the name of our Lord Jesus Christ I adjure you to
depart from this place and not dare to harm anyone here."
He then rowed with speed to the shore and told Columban
about what he had heard. The whole sleeping community
was aroused by the bell. Before they had finished chanting
psalms, they heard the voices passing from summit to
summit of the mountains in a great fearful receding wail.
Then, the last echo faded, the silence of the night came
down.

It is possible that the priests or ministers of the old
religion had endeavoured to frighten the monks and rouse
the people against them; it is possible that the story preserves a vivid memory of the sounds heard out on the silent
lake by Gall the fisherman when the Alamannians held
their ritual festivals on the lakeside or up in the clearings
on the wooded hills. The memory of the bell that called
the sleeping monks to the little oratory of St. Aurelia was
preserved for a long time. Until 1786, a very ancient bell
called the Bell of St. Columban was preserved in a church
in Bregenz; it was then presented to the famous monastery
of St. Gall.

Gall was a good fisherman and the monks must have been
good farmers, but neither his skill nor their experience
could safeguard the community against seasons of scarcity
when the weather went against the crops, or one year's
harvest was eaten up before the next year's was reaped.
Seasonal scarcity was part of the pattern of their lives, a test
they could endure by trusting in the providence of God and

tightening the cords of their habits. While they were in Bregenz there came, as Jonas tells, a time of hard want. They ran out of food. For three days they had nothing to eat. It can only have been a scarcity that afflicted the whole neighbourhood where surely they had found friends among the people. When they were weak from hunger, a huge flock of birds arrived such as had come to the needy Israelites and settled on the monastery land. It was the monk Eustasius, later abbot of Luxeuil, who told the story in detail to Jonas. He told how Columban had ordered them to praise God and then to capture this "manna" of birds which remained for several days. The birds had such a wonderful flavour that it surpassed the food of kings. On the fourth day, after the birds had departed and the monks had fed so memorably on the roasted wild-fowl, a bishop of some neighbouring city sent food to the monastery.

From about the same period Jonas picked up another story, his informant being Chagnoald, afterwards bishop of Laon. Chagnoald was frequently Columban's minister or attendant in the wilderness of the forest to which they used to retire for solitary prayer and fasting. The cell was a cave. On these occasions they had nothing to eat except wild apples, a poor and bitter food even for fasting monks. One day about mealtime, which was in the early afternoon, Columban told Chagnoald to collect some of the fruit. When Chagnoald reached the trees he found a very hungry bear wandering among the brushwood and biting off the apples the monks needed so badly. He reported to the abbot, and for his pains he was ordered to return and divide the wild orchard into two sections, one for themselves and the other for the bear. The wild beast was

obedient. As long as Columban remained in these parts, the
bear confined himself to his allotted trees and never crossed
into the territory of the monks!

4

It is a simple story, one over which childlike men and
children could nod their heads in wonder. One of many
similar stories about Irish monks at home in Ireland or
wandering on the Continent, it signified a temporary restoration through sanctity of man's lost brotherly dominion
over the beasts and the birds. Such tales would become the
lore of the Middle Ages, and some commentators have professed to see in them the beginnings of that tender regard
for animals, that spirit of fraternity, which the world was to
remember as one of the golden gifts of St. Francis of Assisi.

Beasts may have been biddable, but not men. The monks
had overthrown idols and made some converts, but they
had not conquered all the country folk, the *pagani,* who
resented their presence and their preaching. Enmity had
not died when the echoes faded into the silence of the
night over the lake. Some of the country folk, as Walafrid
wrote, began to stir up hatred and conspire for the removal
of the monks. But as long as the monks lived under the protection of King Theudebert of Austrasia, they were comparatively safe. Columban himself cannot have believed
that this protection would last for long. Had he not on
three different occasions set a term of three years to the
dominion of Burgundy and Austrasia, with victory for King
Clothair of Neustria? He was already thinking of taking to

the road once more and entering into the territories of the Slavs, but it was a plan he put aside. Across the mountains lay Italy, the kingdom of the Lombards, the patchwork of Roman provinces shrunken to the coastal areas, and the highway to Rome which he had desired to visit so that he might kneel before the pope and pray at the tomb of the Apostles. Italy has become like a promised land.

The term of the reiterated prophecy was nearly completed. Alarmed for the sake of the king who had befriended him, Columban decided to visit Theudebert and persuade him from engaging in war. There was other counsel that the king needed. In the mad repetitive tragedy of the Merovingian house, Theudebert had killed his wife in a fit of anger and then married the inevitable young girl.

According to some biographers, Columban could not have had time to make the long journey from Bregenz to Metz and back again, but Jonas is quite clear about this visit to the doomed king, and about what Columban personally asked him to do. What he asked was very strange. He begged him to put away his pride and become a cleric, to place himself under the rule of the Church and not to risk his eternal life as well as his earthly kingdom. Columban spoke in the presence of the courtiers—a lean old man wrinkled like a dried grape, leaning on a staff—and if he had been a travelling tumbler or a buffoon acting out coarse jokes for these coarse-grained men, he could not have aroused more laughter. Who had ever heard of a Merovingian becoming a cleric of his own free will! Many Merovingian queens and princesses had given themselves to lives of prayer, cared for the poor, founded convents, and tried to keep some sort of sanity and sweetness in drunken,

sweaty, murderous households that were so often shaken
with outbursts of passion like gales. But that was woman's
work! These men in Theudebert's court scorned this monk,
but the monk said:

"If he does not become a cleric of his own free will,
in a short while he will become one by force."

Columban returned to Bregenz. The kingdoms of Gaul
began to echo with rumours of war as the royal horsemen
rode across the territories to muster armies. Brunhilde and
Theuderich worked well. They got from King Clothair of
Neustria a promise of neutrality. In the spring of 612, they
gathered an immense army at the ancient Roman fortress
town of Langres on the Marne and, moving northeastwards,
drove before them whatever opposition they met, wasting
the Austrasian land, and ejected the Austrasian garrison
from the fortress town of Toul. During the investment of
Toul, Theudebert's army had come up, too late to preserve
the fortress that guarded this hollow in the great hills and
the valley of the Moselle. Theudebert's army broke and
thousands of his best fighters were killed, while he himself,
pursued, fled on down the valley through Metz and northeastwards to Cologne. This was no brief campaign to be
resolved by a single victory or defeat. With his back to the
Rhine, he sent the remnants of his staff to gather another
army, Saxons and Thuringians and fighters from the other
side of the river. All during that summer, the armies of
Theuderich advanced, at last conquering Austrasia and
avenging the indignities the old queen had suffered. The
closer they came to Cologne, the nearer approached the
fulfilment of another whorled Merovingian pattern. It was
like a grim and bloody Germanic tale with a motif of in-

evitable doom in an inevitable place. Some twenty-five miles southwest of Cologne, nearly halfway between Aix-la-Chapelle and Bonn, there lay the meeting place of the two fratricidal brothers, and there can have been few Franks who met in the slaughter of that day who did not know that this was the place in which victory had been given more than a century previously to the primal Merovingian, Clovis, in whose sons and grandsons and great-grandsons were reflected his warring virtues and vices. It was the field of Tolbiac, Zülpich, that was again to witness a most terrible battle. It was terrible in the slaughter and in the pursuit that came after. "So close was the fight and so frightful the butchery," wrote a chronicler, "the corpses of the slain had no room to fall but were held upright among the living fighters." Theudebert's second army broke, fled, and died in the headlong pursuit by Theuderich's cavalry. Theuderich himself rode on, entered Cologne, looted his brother's treasury, and had his little son put to death. Theudebert himself had escaped across the Rhine with a few followers, a ruined king who had lost all Austrasia and Alsace and Alamannia, but the escape was brief. He was overtaken by Count Bertechar, the same man who had ridden into Luxeuil to banish the Irish monks, captured, and brought back to Chalon to Queen Brunhilde. It is possible she wished to save his life, for she had him tonsured and put into a monastery. Did he recall Columban then, or a few days later when he was taken out from his last foretold asylum and killed?

He had, at least, Columban's prayers in his death agonies. On the day of the battle, Columban was alone in the forest solitude with Chagnoald. While he was sitting on the

trunk of a fallen tree, a rotten oak, reading and meditating,
he was suddenly oppressed by a heavy drowsiness, and he
had a vision like a dream of what was happening hundreds
of miles away to the north between the two kings. As soon
as he came to himself out of this trance-like sleep, he called
Chagnoald and told him he had seen the slaughter of the
battle with the blood of many men flowing on the ground.

"My father," Chagnoald said, "give Theudebert the help
of your prayers that he may defeat our common enemy,
Theuderich."

"You give advice," the abbot replied, "that is foolish and
contrary to religion. That is not how the Lord wished it,
Who asked us to pray for our enemies. What He wishes
to be done with these men is in the keeping of the Just
Judge."

Chagnoald did not forget the day. Later he inquired
about the time of the battle and found that things had happened just as Columban had seen them.

Less than six months later Columban's prophecy about
the Merovingians was almost fulfilled when Theuderich,
still in his early manhood, died of dysentery in Metz. There
still remained the last stage of fulfilment that would make
Clothair ruler of three kingdoms, uniting under his crown
the tormented patrimony of Clovis; but before that would
happen, Columban and most of his monks would be far
away.

The defeat of King Theudebert meant the end of the
security in which the monks had lived in Bregenz. The
country folk could now work openly against them. Some of
them went to the duke of the country, Gunzo by name, and
complained that the monks had interfered with the hunt-

ing in his woods. There was probably some truth in the
charge, but the comparatively few acres cleared and tilled
by the monks could have made little difference to the
game. What the country folk wanted was banishment of the
strangers who had offended against the old gods. They had
their wish. Duke Gunzo became inflamed with wrath, and
he sent messengers with orders for the monks to quit the
neighbourhood. It should have been enough for the *pagani*,
but they were still dissatisfied. With a meanness that is all
the more vile because it waited slyly until now for action,
they stole a cow belonging to the monks and drove it off
into the depths of the forest. Two of the monks tracked
them and were ambushed by the robbers, who killed them
and left the bodies lying there. Columban became uneasy
when the return of two of the brethren was delayed hour
after hour, and he sent other monks to search for them.
They, too, followed the tracks and found the dead men.
They laid the bodies on their shoulders and carried them
back to the cloister.

This violence and Duke Gunzo's order of banishment
meant the end of the community at Bregenz. The monks
had come to love the place. They grieved, as Walafrid
wrote. What they grieved for was the spaciousness and the
peace that are the beatitudes of a huge expanse of inland
water, the mountains lifting up the snow to the clouds, the
little church they had reclaimed, the populous forests, and
the clearings where, as with men whose expectations are
measured in years of stability, they had planted fruit-trees.
Columban tried to comfort them, saying, "My brothers, we
have indeed found a golden shell here, but it is one that
harboured venomous reptiles." There was bitter resent-

ment in his comfort, but there was also that surge of valour, incredible in so old a man, who now proposed that they should travel with him across the mountain passes and down into Italy, to the country ruled by Agilulf, king of the Lombards.

We do not know how many monks accompanied him. By inference, we can say that one of his companions was Attala, who walked this long last road into Italy, and that another was Sigisbert, who left them while they were still in the mountains. We can guess that others of the community undertook missionary work, and that some, including Eustasius, returned then or not much later to Luxeuil. But of one monk we can say definitely that he remained behind after a brief dialogue with the abbot which, centuries later, can still disconcert, puzzle and even hurt sympathetic commentators. The monk was Gall.

It is Walafrid Strabo who tells the story. Jonas is silent. He must have heard the story in some form from Gall or some of the other monks whom he met and questioned, and he must have found the wintry harshness of the scene hard to take. Columban was his hero, just as Gall was Walafrid's; and a writer of his mood and time did not speak ill, or at least, did not point to what looked like a defect in the holy founder he had been commissioned to celebrate. The story is brief, hardly more than a few lines in Walafrid's book.

When the time came for the departure of the monks, Gall fell suddenly ill of a fever. He threw himself at the abbot's feet, saying he was suffering from a severe illness and was unable for the journey. Columban said to him:

"Brother, I know that now it seems a heavy burden to you to suffer hardship and weariness for my sake. So be it, but before I depart I command you that so long as I live in the body you shall not take it on you to celebrate Mass."

Whether the words were spoken in a whisper, a murmur, a calm natural tone or in a shout, they come with an unexpected and shocking force. It is only too easy to interpret them as an expression of violent harshness, or of an old man's anger. The command was fearful: as long as the abbot lived, and God knew how long, Gall the priest was not to say Mass. For the man professionally poor in spirit, the penalty meant spiritual impoverishment. As if he were making an excuse for the harshness, Walafrid wrote that Columban thought Gall was held back by love of the place in which he had laboured and by fear of the fatigue of the long journey. But did Walafrid—or the silent Jonas —ever meditate on what that command must have done to Columban?

They were thoughtful men. We can be fairly sure they did meditate and in the mind's eye follow that old man who, staff in hand and accompanied by a few monks, struck off on the path among the trees that would lead to the southward road, the tracks across the high mountain passes, and the cold pouring down from the icy ramparts of rock in the thin air. If the mind's eye saw tears streaming down that face which hunger and hardship had shaped almost to the sunken contours of the skull, then it probably saw some of the truth of the story. For Columban and Gall were brothers with affinities that could never be inherited from a mother's womb. By the bonds of the charity that had held them together in a common life, with its shared daily routine of prayer, work, learning, hardships, adventures, disasters, journeys, dangers, joys, and the mutual fashion-

ing of mind by mind, they were brothers in Christ. But it
was precisely one of the rules of that common life was at
stake when Columban commanded the monks to depart
from Bregenz and Gall answered that he was unable to go.

What obedience to the abbot signified in that common
life, we already know. "But up to what measure is obedience to be limited?" Columban had written, and Gall had
learned and read and learned again. "Up to death it is
surely enjoined," Columban had answered, "since for us
Christ obeyed the Father up to death." *Usque ad mortem!*
It was an absolute demand which was quite in accord with
the recurrent image of the monk as soldier, always ready
for battle even if it brought death. The small army was
now being driven from yet another stronghold; it was retreat; there was a command issued and personal feelings
had to be discounted. There was danger if the monks hated,
and danger if they loved. Hatred and love were real, but
peace perished in hatred, and integrity perished in love. On
that day when Columban set off, neither peace nor integrity perished, and there was no hatred but there was much
love.

We know that much from, at least, what happened to
Gall.

5

Gall was a sick man and suddenly he was alone. The
track among the trees was empty. The cells were empty.
The fruit trees stood for other hands to pick. He went down
to the lake, and gathering his nets, the big and the little

that he had woven, he placed them in a boat and rowed with the fever burning in him along the shore to Arbon and the house of their old friend, Willimar the priest. It must have taken him a whole day of pulling on the oars. To Willimar he offered the nets, and he told him, weeping, what had happened to the monastery, and how he himself was ill. He begged Willimar to take him under his care. He hardly needed to ask that hospitable priest, who brought him to a house close to the church and put him under the care of two of his clerics, Magnoald and Theodore, men who would be later remembered in Bavaria as saints and founders of monasteries.

When Gall recovered, he spoke to that deacon, Hiltibod, the hunter and fisherman who knew the wilderness, and he asked him if he had ever discovered any place in the desolation where there was plenty of water and a piece of level ground for tillage.

"I am filled," he said, "with a burning desire to pass whatever days I have left in some retreat."

Hiltibod knew of many likely spots where there were many streams. "But," he warned, "it's a wild and fearsome place, full of high mountains with narrow winding gorges and haunted by wild beasts. Besides deer and other harmless animals, there are bears, boars, and wolves beyond number and very savage."

This was the country that Gall desired. With fishing nets and a wallet of food, he and Hiltibod set off one daybreak into the wilderness, and in the afternoon when it was the usual monastic time to break the fast. Hiltibod said:

"Father, it's now time to break our fast. Let us refresh ourselves with a little bread and water so that we may be better able for the rest of the journey."

"Let you eat, my son," Gall said. "Take what food your body needs. I will taste nothing till the Lord shows me the spot where I must stay."

"If," Hiltibod answered, " we are to be partners in hardship, let us be partners in consolation."

The early evening of the mountains was falling as they hurried on. Their path struck the course of a stream called the Steinach that runs down to Lake Constance. They followed its course along the darkening banks, tracking the waters that tumbled white under the pale evening sky, until they entered a rocky gorge where the stream pitched in turmoil into a pool. They stood and watched in the damp cold air and saw fish. They cast the nets and were fortunate. While Hiltibod lit a fire, striking it from flint, iron and tinder, broiled some fish and laid the cakes of bread on the wallet, Gall retired a short distance to pray. As he was treading through a tangle of briars, he was tripped, and he fell on the ground. Hiltibod ran to lift him, but he said: "Let me lie." A psalm, one of the endlessly repeated prayers that had become almost as instinctive as a cry of joy or pain, echoed in his mind. "This shall be my rest for ever. Here will I stay, for I have chosen it."

Where he had fallen, he knelt and prayed for a while.

There must have been a hazel tree growing nearby, because he snapped off a branch, fashioned it into a cross and fixed it into the earth. From his neck he had a small leather satchel hanging on a strap. It contained relics of Mary, the Mother of God (so Walafrid wrote), of St. Maurice the martyr of the Theban Legion, and of Bishop Desiderius, who had been killed by King Theuderich's men. He suspended this satchel from the hazel cross and called to Hiltibod to pray with him that Jesus Christ, for the honour of

Our Lady, the martyrs and confessors, might not spurn his desire to prepare a habitation in the neighbourhood.

Only the sky and the foaming river held any light now. The fire glowed where the fish was being cooked. The trees that were touched on trunk and bough by the red glow of the embers became ghosts of themselves as the darkness filled the gorge. At last, the two men ate the food, and then strewed branches and grass on the ground as bedding for the night.

Neither slept. They may have been overfatigued by the long day's journey. The cold night air in the mountains can bring on an agony of numbness when bodily energy and heat are low. There was, besides, the muffled thunder of the plunging Steinach in the gorge. But Gall kept himself awake and alert for a reason. He wanted to pray again, alone. He watched till he thought Hiltibod was asleep. Then he rose, and going to the hazel cross where the satchel hung, he knelt with arms outstretched in the old Irish manner of the cross-vigil. All the time, the prostrate deacon was watching with the eye of a hawk. Because he knew the wilderness and had hunted through it with keen ear as well as sharp eye, he probably first heard the animal that came down the mountainside and padded through the under-brush to lumber round the fire for the scraps of bread and fish. It was a hungry bear. Hiltibod lay still. Gall saw the bear at last and said: "In the Lord's name, I command you to take up a log and throw it on the fire."

Only the watchful deacon could have told the story of what happened.

The bear turned away, found a log and threw it on the embers. Gall went to the food-wallet and took out an un-

broken loaf, which he gave to the bear, saying, "In the
Lord's name, I command you to leave this valley. You are
free to range the hills and mountains around here as long
as you do no harm to man or beast in this place."

Hiltibod got up from his bed and threw himself at
Gall's feet, crying out, "Now I know for sure the Lord is
with you, because even the wild beasts obey you."

"Take heed," Gall answered, "that you tell no man about
this till you see God's glory."

Whatever the injunction meant, Hiltibod did not obey.
Not many days later, he left Gall alone in the wilderness, returned to Arbon and told Willimar the priest and others at
the dinner-table about what he had witnessed on the bank
of the Steinach; and so the story began its travels through
the centuries, by written and spoken word, and by pig-
ment, wood, stone and ivory. The bear carrying the log,
Gall giving bread, the deacon pretending to be asleep, and
the hazel cross with the hanging satchel of relics: this was
the scene which was carved as one of the panels on the tab-
let of ivory which formed the back cover of the famous
Long Gospel, so called from its shape.

The library of the monastery of St. Gall cherished it,
holding it as one of its chief treasures. It was carved in the
ninth century by the monk Tutilo, a hearty jovial man who
could fight as well as he could pray. He was also an accomplished musician and painter who often travelled far
to meet the demands for his services. God gave him a wonderful pair of hands. From his fingers, it was once related,
light streamed as he carved a figure of Our Lady in low-
relief in a church in Metz. His tongue was so ready in
repartee that a king cursed the person, whoever he was, that

had turned such a man into a monk! The ivory tablets Tutilo used for the carving had belonged, according to tradition, to no less a personage than the Emperor Charlemagne, who kept them beside his bed for scratching letters on. Caesar's ciphers were erased to make way for the image of a saint. In the delicate, spirited figures carved by the happy monk, and in the gold and silver and red illumination of the Gospels that were deliberately copied to fit the ivory binding, there is a bright touch of the poetry that was to be part of the long history of the monastery.

It was a history that covered twelve centuries under the Benedictine Rule which succeeded the Columbanian. In the extended procession of abbots there were many supremely able and illustrious men: Gozbert, who commissioned Walafrid Strabo to write about St. Gall; Grimald, Hartmuot; Solomon of Ramschwag, who was a princely Christian humanist; Ekkehard, the fourth of the name; Burkhard, Ulrich Rösch—scholars, poets, teachers and builders who made the abbey prosper, fostered the schools where "St. Gall's chickens" nested, and produced scholars and artists like Notker Balbulus, Ratpert, and Tutilo. The school of music, especially under Notker, became famous. The library became one of the fabulous treasures of Europe. But all this belongs to another story which began with a monk falling among briars and forming a cross from a hazel branch.

The morning after that night beside the river, Gall and Hiltibod continued along a valley until they came to a level wooded place enclosed by the hills between the conjunction of the Steinach and the Irr. This was the destination. Here Gall would set up a monastic settlement. From here he

would go down to Lake Constance to heal the daughter of
the same Duke Gunzo who had banished Columban and
the monks and so earn a permanent, protective and generous gratitude. When the duke and others begged Gall to
accept the rank of bishop, he replied:

"As long as my lord and father Columban is alive, the
ministry of the altar is forbidden to me. I will not accept it
without his leave. Therefore, the authority you wish to give
me is a burden I may not bear."

Later, when he was brought to the town of Arbon with
a great treasure the duke had given him, he called all the
poor and needy and distributed the gifts among them. One
of his disciples, Magnoald, on seeing this alms-giving, said
to him, "My father, I have here a costly silver vessel, beautifully chased. If you wish, I will keep it back so that we
may make vessels for the altar."

"My son," Gall answered, "remember the words the holy
apostle, Peter, spoke to the palsied man who begged for
money: 'Gold and silver have I none.' For fear you fall
from this good example, give the vessel you hold to the
poor. My blessed teacher, Columban, is accustomed to offer
the sacrifice of the Mass in iron vessels because it is said
that our Saviour was fastened to the cross with iron nails."

At such remembrance and obedience, Columban would
have wept.

CHAPTER 7

The Lombard Court

COLUMBAN was far away, down in the plains of Italy.

With Attala and Sigisbert, he had taken the direct road from Bregenz to Chur where there was a choice of routes southwards through the overwhelming confusion of mountains. It was probably here, at Chur, that Sigisbert left the party, either by command or by his own wish to retire into solitude. He made his way in a westerly direction up a river valley, found the place he wanted on a sheer mountainside, and built himself a hermitage and there, as was inevitable where the sons of Luxeuil settled down, he presently found himself with disciples and then with the monastic community from which was developed the celebrated abbey of Disentis, almost at the foot of the St. Gotthard. Columban and Attala had continued southwards. The community was breaking up, but it was like a fruit breaking to scatter incredibly fertile seed far away with the wind.

We do not know on what track the two men marched, or which passes they crossed, but conjectures can fortunately be limited. Their route probably wound up over the Septimar, one of the oldest roads along which Roman legions and officials had come. The going was mostly sound and good, except in the marshy places and at the fords where floods could make streams vicious and dangerous. The ascent from the northern side up to some seven thousand, five hundred feet is not too difficult, though it may have been arduous enough for that old man who drove himself with less pity than he ever gave to his monks. A man driving himself hard on that track can find himself gulping for deeper breaths of the rarefied air, needle-sharp with the cold blowing off the fields and peaks of ice, or find his clothes heavy and beaded with droplets of the mists that can shut off the world. At any rate, Columban disappears from all narratives, like a man temporarily lost from sight, and then he is suddenly found in the Italian sun at the court of a king in Milan: *Rex Gentis Lombardorum:* the King of the Lombard People.

All during his life as a pilgrim, it had been Columban's choice and fate to deal with Germanic peoples. He encountered them in varying phases of cultural assimilation to the ruined Roman *civilitas* and in different conditions of religious obedience to the Church, whose missionaries had gone out along the Roman roads and used the language of the Romans. Some, like the Franks, had been *foederati* of the Roman power; others, like the heathen Alamannians, squatted unconquered in the shattered towns they had overrun. Roman ideas and Christian teaching were slowly transforming all of them with their immense energies and virtues into the new peoples who would be the very stuff of the world of the Middle Ages.

Columban was conscious of Roman ideas in the literature that he carried in his memory and in a few beloved books. Rome spoke to him with the calm insistent murmur of magisterial voices which modified the Latin he wrote in verse, sermon or letter. But his schooling in Ireland in the language and literature of Rome, whether the voices were Virgil's, Ovid's, or of Jerome's Vulgate or of the Old Latin Bible, had not so completely absorbed his sense of loyalty as to make him look on the Germanic peoples with the supercilious regard of proud sophisticated Roman citizens. He had a native sympathy with the outlanders that Romans called barbarians. The texture of their culture was similar to that of his own people's. It was not an urban but a rural texture, a thing hardly processed after it had left the forests and the plains, like the oily homespun wool of the habit he wore in Bangor. It depended on strong and accurately noted strands of kinship; it cherished the family-group as the basic pattern; and its strongest colour was the heroism of the warrior who was celebrated in sagas for his valour, and elected as king during the frequent periods of war.

Once more, this time in the lush meadows and wheat fields of the plains of northern Italy, Columban came among a Germanic people whose tenacious memories, filled with recitals of violent deeds, blood-feuds, vengeance and battles, could go back to migrations in the vast forests beyond the Alps, beyond the Danube, and even beyond the cold northern seas. Beyond the Alps, they had been drifting and settling in almost every generation for centuries, drifting and settling in the gigantic southward migrations against which the Roman power, directed from Constantinople, tried in vain to fight, bargain, and make treaties. By the end of the fifth century, this people called Lombards by Roman chroniclers dominated Pannonia and became Rome's neighbours on the Danube. They became Chris-

tians of a sort, but their beliefs were Arian. Warfare was
a means of livelihood. Migration had never allowed them to
practise more than a primitive form of agriculture; and in
any case, being warriors who scorned labour, they used
slaves and subject peoples for the work of the fields. But
in Pannonia they came under pressure from the Avars, a
fierce, land-hungry tribe of Asiatic origin, and their independence was threatened.

Once more they migrated, and it was for the last time.
They knew the promise of the land they lusted after, Italy,
because many of their warriors had fought against invading
Goth and Frank for what they could pick up in loot and
pay in the imperial armies of Belisarius and Narses. Those
very wars of liberation had filled the northern plain with a
melancholy desolation, with what Paul the Deacon, historian of the Lombards, had described as "primeval silence
and solitude." There was land for the taking. When Columban was still in Bangor, a monk in his late twenties, the
whole Lombard people crossed the Carinthian Alps in the
summer of 568. The long trailing army of displaced persons, warriors, women, children, slaves, waggons, horses,
oxen and other livestock, streamed down from the passes
and began, like a flood, to spread out over the Venetian
plain. Year after year the flood moved, settling in pools
that were to be Lombardic for ever after. They took city
after city, Cividale, Aquileia, Milan, Pavia, Verona; surged
up the valley of the Po; drove southwards down the Apennines; and ate into the entire imperial pattern till the imperial power was faced with the complicated task of defending the coastal fragments, the Exarchate of Ravenna,
Liguria, the Roman territory and Calabria.

Previous invaders of Italy had considered themselves, or had been tactfully considered, as partners in empire, guests who would conform in some way or other. The Lombards, on the contrary, looked on the inhabitants as subjects, landlords to be dispossessed, women to be used as concubines, officials, craftsmen and farm-workers to be treated as slaves. Every free Lombard was both soldier and landowner. Church property was seized without scruple. By the time Columban founded Luxeuil, the Lombard was firmly established, and the more powerful leaders had carved out duchies for themselves. By the time he descended from the Alpine heights to the plains that were to be forever called Lombardy, the invaders were acknowledging the rule of one of the wisest of their kings, Agilulf, duke of Turin. He was the first of his race to be crowned with the famous Iron Crown, a hoop of gold around the interior of which was a strip of iron, said to have been a nail of the true Cross, brought from the Holy Land by the Empress Helena.

Agilulf had married Theudelinda, the widow of his predecessor, Authari. She was a pious Christian, anxious to see the end of the Arian heresy and to accomplish the conversion of her husband. On his way southward, it is likely that Columban had halted at Monza, three hours easy march north of Milan, and had prayed in the church of St. John which she had founded, and had gazed on the pictures which she had caused to be painted for the palace: pictures that showed Lombard nobles with their hair clipped close at the back of their heads, worn long on the crown and parted in the middle to hang down over the cheeks; with loose linen clothes striped broadly with various colours; and with boots, open almost to the toes but laced crosswise. A Bavarian, she was proud of the race into which she had married; and among the warriors, she was a civilizing force.

Despite the strangeness of scene and people, Columban was in a friendlier country. The warmer air was less trying on his ageing lungs. Jonas says simply that Columban was well received by Agilulf, who offered him the generous choice of settling down wherever he liked in Italy. Many kings in his lifetime had made similar offers. He had accepted. For a while his work, his foundations, had seemingly flourished, but then something had gone wrong, and a king or a queen had turned sourly against him. With a patience and a hope like the undefeatable persistence of the green grass that springs up in a crack in a pavement, covers battlefields and fallen cities, he had started afresh. He had started afresh with the wilderness where the forest floor was thick and intractable with the peaty humus and the knotted root-systems of the centuries. Now, in his seventies, he was being given the choice all over again. He had the support of a king—stubbornly Arian though the king was; and he had the friendship of a queen. She was the second of the two royal women of authority and experience to influence directly the course of his life.

He remained for some time in Milan. True to his nature, he was not inactive. The fact that King Agilulf and his subjects professed the Arian perversion of the Faith was in itself a challenge to his zeal and his powers. He began to write again in the peace of Milan. Jonas tells us that he attacked the Arians and wrote a short learned work in a flowery style against the heresy. This work has never been discovered. It is probable that at this time he composed and delivered his extant series of sermons, in the first of which he emphasizes Catholic teaching concerning the Blessed Trinity. The sermons were in Latin, a language which, it is likely, few Lombards knew when they invaded Italy, but which, in the demands of everyday life among their Latin subjects, they began to favour until the use of Lombard words among the nobles came to be considered as vulgar. Columban's sermons are vigorous and frequently elaborate in sentence construction. Perhaps the texts, of which scholars have disputed the authenticity, were used as guides for the preacher on the great occasions when king and queen, nobles and Lombard people, stood quietly to hear the old monk deepening and renewing their Christian beliefs.

"Let every man," he said, "who wants to be saved, first believe in God the first and the last, one and three, one in substance, three in subsistence, one in power, three in person, one in nature, three in name, one in divinity Who is Father and Son and Holy Spirit, one God, wholly invisible, incomprehensible, ineffable, in Whom is everlasting existence because God the Trinity is eternal, Whose beginning one does not seek, Who has no end, and Who has ever been that which He is and shall be . . . and this is to be held firmly against all heresies, that the one God cannot be divided or separated since that which is the all, has been always as it is. Let there be an end, then, to the venomous and crazy raving of all the heretics. . . ."

. . . . *venenosa et insana omnium hereticorum vesania* . . .

Let there be an end! It was a pious hope, vigorously expressed.

2

The embittered deliriums of heretics were inevitably a cause of grief to the monk who had given so much of his life to missionary work. When heretical beliefs became too subtle and complicated, error ramifying into error in the name of orthodoxy and by an inevitable process of dialectic, a prudent monk would avoid them, keep a tactful silence and seek counsel from the highest authority. Columban was not long in Milan before he found himself involved in an old schism that had riven the Church in Italy and other parts of the West. Prudently, he turned in perplexity to the pope, Boniface IV, for counsel and a decision, but the very terms of the tediously voluminous letter which he wrote to Rome were imprudent. He gave more counsel than he asked for, and the decision he demanded was that the pope should clear himself of a suspicion of heresy. He wrote out of ignorance and out of a deep simplicity about a tortuously complicated affair. This was a patch of the wilderness which could not be cleared easily with spade and axe. The forest floor was thick with the entangled roots and underbrush of several centuries of controversy.

Of the Arian Christians he knew a great deal. He had met them in the flesh among the Germanic tribes. Agilulf and his Lombards were Arians. Columban knew them as believers who did not accept the tradition that the Logos is truly God. He must have known much about the triumph of that heresy during the past in the Eastern Church, among the members of the imperial court, among the subtle

Greek-speaking intellectuals, and in the army. But how much did he know about the interference, willingly accepted and frequently invited, of the emperors in Constantinople, with the business and prerogatives of the Church, with ecclesiastical discipline, the election of bishops, the convening of synods and councils and even the definition of doctrine? Ireland was remote from that secular and spiritual sophistication. It is probably near enough to the truth to say that he did know from travellers and from encounters with ecclesiastics in Gaul how Christian Caesar, hedged about by vestiges of the ancient imperial divinity, had arrogated to himself not only the things that were Caesar's but also many of the things that were God's. Out of this Caesaro-Papist environment came the schism in which Columban, with grief, found himself playing a part he should never have tried to play. His part was a wearying digression in the few years of life he had left.

The causes of the digression must take us back to some years before the birth of Columban. Justinian was Emperor in Constantinople, and Pope Vigilius, creature of the Empress Theodora, sat on the throne of Peter. In Italy, the imperial armies under Belisarius were engaged in a devastating series of campaigns against the Goths. To his vision of a restored empire at peace within and on the frontiers, to his immense practical abilities, his industry and his personal culture, Justinian unfortunately added a taste for theological speculation. He had, indeed, helped his uncle, the previous emperor, to end a schism of some two score years with Rome. He had also helped to rid many vantage points of Monophysites in the Eastern sees, followers of the heresy that had ravaged the peace of the empire for nearly half-a-century. But the Monophysites were not put down so easily. The Arians had denied the eternal Godhead of Christ; the Nestorians, reacting, had rationalized the Incarnate Logos into two natures, two *physes*, the human and the divine, united in a union that was no more than moral; and the Monophysites, concerned to preserve the unity of the person of God the Son, clung to their image of a divine Christ who was not human at all. "One incarnate *physis* of God the Word" was the crucial phrase, a favourite formula of the orthodox St. Cyril of Alexandria that the Monophysites could interpret and use to their own advantage. The Council of Chalcedon had condemned their beliefs in 451. The Emperor Justinian knew how inflexible and fierce was their hostility to the council's decisions. Optimistically, he set about finding a means of reconciliation between them and the Catholics, some sort of theological formula, that magical parchment of the Byzantine Civil Service confronted by religious dispute, which would bring the conflicting parties together in a secular peace. Under his auspices, Catholic and Monophysite bishops met and the old spiralling discussions began all over again.

Another conflict, also religious, now engaged the theologizing emperor's attention. In the province of Palestine a hoary dispute, more ancient than Monophysitism, was resurrected concerning the orthodoxy of certain theories attributed to Origen, then dead for nearly three centuries. Monks in the Palestinian monasteries, among whom was one Theodore Askidas, had begun to discuss with passion and even with violence theories of the eternity of the material world, the pre-existence of the human soul, a quasi-pantheistic destiny of man, and a final universal redemp-

tion by which all created things including the devil would
be saved. As had happened again and again in previous
religious conflicts, disputants took their cases to Caesar.
One of the deputies was Theodore Askidas. In that court in
which the emperor dabbled in theology and the empress
tended to encourage Monophysites as well as the fanciful
and the bizarre in religion, Theodore Askidas got more
than a fair hearing. Indeed, he did very well for himself.
He was made bishop of Caesarea in Cappadocia, but he continued to live on at court, a confidant of Justinian's. Meanwhile, a synod had been called in Palestine, at Gaza, to deal
with the Origenists. Among the dignitaries present was the
permanent ambassador or *apocrisiarius* of the Roman see
at the court. He was the deacon, Pelagius. He was the
friend and, in fact, the strength of Pope Vigilius. At the
synod he encouraged the afflicted abbots to take action
against the Origenist monks, and when he returned to the
court, he persuaded Justinian to issue an edict in condemnation of the Origenist theories. A formulary was also
issued which all bishops and monastic heads were obliged
to sign.

It was signed by Theodore Askidas. He had lost face.
Foxily, he began to conspire for the restoration of favour
and for the dislodgment of Pelagius. He played on the
emperor's intellectual vanity and theological ambition.
He proposed a plan for the reconciliation of the Catholics
and the Monophysites. It was a subtle plan. It would not
even suggest that anything of the Chalcedon decisions
should be repudiated. It would merely propose the condemnation of three men who had been in their graves for
more than a hundred years.

The first of those three dead men was Theodore, bishop of Mopsuestia, the most celebrated of the Antiochean (two *physes*) theologians. He had been teacher of Nestorius the heretic. Next, there was another pupil, Theodoret of Cyrrhus, a bishop who had revised his master's theories and had most assuredly become orthodox. The third was yet another pupil, Ibas, bishop of Edessa, who with Theodoret had suffered deposition and false excommunication in the troubles provoked by the Monophysite monk, Eutyches, and that ecclesiastical gangster, Dioscoros, bishop of Alexandria. Both had been restored to their sees by the Council of Chalcedon. What evil, then, did Theodore Askidas find in them?

He declared that they had, in reality, been Nestorians, and that Theodore, bishop of Mopsuestia, had been the spiritual father of Nestorianism. There was some truth in the charges. If the three men were to be condemned, it would prove to the suspicious Monophysites that the Catholics were not Nestorians. It would also prove that what the Council of Ephesus settled in 431 when it condemned Nestorius had not been undone by Chalcedon, which in 451 reinstated the supposedly Nestorian bishops of Cyrrhus and Edessa. The condemnation of the three men was to be based on the written word: on all the writings of Theodore of Mopsuestia; on those writings of Theodoret of Cyrrhus which had been directed again St. Cyril during the Nestorian controversy; and on a letter written by Ibas to a Persian bishop. The plan was ingenious, looked sound and appealed to the emperor. In 544 he issued an edict in which the three matters of condemnation, the Three Chapters as they were called, were anathematized.

In a sense, that edict was the beginning of schism, the slight tremor in the ground that foretold earthquake.

The *apocrisiarius,* Pelagius, refused to sign the imperial anathema. The patriarchs of Constantinople, Antioch and Alexandria, the three great Eastern sees, agreed to sign on condition that Pope Vigilius should sign also. But here was a dilemma for a man who was least fitted to deal with dilemmas. Vigilius, weak, indecisive and one of the most pitiful of popes, had been placed on the throne of St. Peter by the intrigues of his friend and patroness, the pro-Monophysite Empress Theodora.

The points of the dilemma must be noted. More than any other, Chalcedon had been a pope's council. Through St. Leo I, Rome had spoken clearly and decisively about the relations of the human and the divine in Jesus Christ. The council had reinstated Theodoret and Ibas in their sees upon their express repudiation of Nestorianism. Moreover, the allegedly offending letter of Ibas to the Persian bishop, now condemned by imperial edict, had been read to the council and the Roman legates had pronounced it orthodox. If Pope Vigilius were now to sign and so condemn Theodoret and Ibas for heresies of which they had been cleared, then it would appear that he would also be obliquely but certainly repudiating the council itself. A pope repudiating a pope's council! But how could Pope Vigilius escape from granting the request of the emperor and empress?

He temporized. He could claim as excuse that the Goths were almost at the gates of Rome for yet another siege. The delay displeased Theodora. In November, 545—Columban was a child in the island at the edge of the world—she had the pope seized, shipped off to Sicily, and a year later brought to Constantinople. During those months in Sicily he learned of the storm which was blowing up in the West against the imperial edict. He tried to make a stand against the emperor, and he was supported by Pelagius. One by one, the Eastern bishops after private interviews with Justinian wrote to the pope to tell him that they favoured the condemnation. Vigilius broke, but not completely. On Holy Saturday, 548, he issued the *Iudicatum,* his own public condemnation of the Three Chapters, but to the chagrin of the pro-Monophysites, he made reservations to preserve the essential teaching of Chalcedon.

The West deserted him. In Rome, his own deacons led the opposition against him. It was suggested to him that the West did not understand, that a General Council to be held at Constantinople might help to instruct the Western bishops. Both the edict and the *Iudicatum* were withdrawn. A bargain was made. Pope and emperor pledged themselves to keep silent until the council should meet, and the pope bound himself on oath to Justinian that he would do his utmost at the council to condemn the Three Chapters.

During the three years that followed pending the council, the emperor broke his pledge of silence. Theodore Askidas was at his elbow. A new edict condemned the Three Chapters. Then something like courage, stimulated by Pelagius, rose in the heart of the temporizing pope. He protested and excommunicated Askidas, and then had to flee for safety from arrest to the church of St. Peter in the capital. Soldiers were sent after him to break down the locked doors and take him. The mob gathered. Inside, Vigilius waited for that howling violence to burst about his

ears. The doors were forced. The soldiers and the mob
surged in, and many hands grasped at Pope Vigilius.
Though eighty years of age, he resisted strongly, wrapped
his arms around the altar columns and clung fiercely as
the columns shook and trembled. In the mob, pity for his
age and reverence for his office began to stir. As the altar
columns collapsed and the dust and debris showered on the
defiant old man, the mob turned in rage on the soldiers,
who fled for their lives. During the night, Pope Vigilius
escaped by way of the rooftops, crossed the Bosporus and
took refuge at Chalcedon in the same basilica in which, a
century previously, the bishops had sat in council to ap-
plaud the words of another pope with cheers.

There was an immense reaction in favour of Vigilius.
Peace of a sort was made, and the new edict which had
broken the pledged silence was withdrawn. Meanwhile, the
emperor prepared for the council to be held at Constantinople by eliminating the names of all the bishops from the
West who were likely to oppose the desired condemnation
of the Three Chapters. Again Vigilius saw with dismay that
he would have to stand alone. Again he hedged and Pelagius tried to make him stand firm. Finally, he declared that
he would give his own decision independently of the council's.

The council met in 553. All the bishops present, except
for a few Africans and Italians, were Greeks. They did what
the emperor asked them to do. Vigilius resisted at first, but
in the end he solemnly recognized the condemnation. The
writings of Theodore, Theodoret and Ibas were anathematized. Only then was the pope allowed to face homewards to

his see. He had been absent nine years and he would never see it. In 555, this most unhappy man died at Syracuse.

Now Pelagius, the source of the pope's courage and strength, was himself in trouble. As soon as the council ended, he was placed in a monastic prison and cut off from the pope's advisers. Secretly, he issued inflammatory statements against the council's decisions. To the bishops of the West he wrote that senile Vigilius had been the victim of imperial coercion, which was quite true. Suddenly, for reasons not now known, he turned about and faced the other way. He accepted the decisions of Constantinople. He, too, condemned the Three Chapters.

He became the emperor's choice for the throne of Peter. As such, he set off for Rome. Only two bishops could be found willing to officiate at his consecration, and a priest supplied for the third. In his profession of faith, however, he declared that he believed with Chalcedon and St. Leo, that he held as orthodox all whom that council and pope had so held, including Theodoret and Ibas. He made no mention of the Council of Constantinople nor of Vigilius nor of the dealings between himself and Justinian. Coldly and resentfully he was accepted. He was suspect. Before they would recognize him, the bishops of Gaul demanded from him a satisfactory statement of his orthodoxy. The sees of Milan and Aquileia and their suffragans, and other north Italian bishops, refused obstinately to enter into communion. It was a terrible confused inheritance. He tried to explain that when he, standing behind Vigilius, had defended the Three Chapters, he had been in agreement with the majority of the bishops, and that when he changed his mind, he changed with the same majority. The hun-

dreds of bishops of Africa, Illyricum and the East had condemned the Three Chapters. It would be foolish of him to
ignore their authority. But his explanation was given little
heed. So, there was schism.

It has been pointed out that later scholars, viewing the
whole complicated affair calmly, can distinguish between
what Chalcedon did in 451 about Theodoret and Ibas and
what Constantinople said about them in 553. Chalcedon reinstated them when they gave guarantees of their orthodoxy. Constantinople condemned the Nestorian writings
which they themselves had repudiated. That is the long
view denied the men engaged in,or directly affected by, the
wretched impassioned business.

There was schism in the West, gaping wide like a zigzag
fissure in the ground after an earthquake. It took time to
fill in the fissure. Pope Gregory and the popes who succeeded him waited patiently on time by adopting a policy
of silence. For too long, words had been like weapons. The
schismatics, especially in northern Italy where they were
encouraged by the Lombard ruleis, were still only too
prompt to accuse the papacy of the errors they attributed
to Vigilius and Pelagius. But Pope Gregory's policy produced good effects. It won over Constantius, bishop of
Milan, but three of his suffragans refused to follow him into
communion. Queen Theudelinda stood with the suffragans.

Such was the religious atmosphere into which Columban
entered when he came down the mountain roads into Italy,
the place to which he had so long desired to go. He was
drawn into the controversy. Why and how did he allow
himself to enter the conflict?

3

Jonas is silent about the whole affair. He presents us with his most tantalizing reticence. It may be fanciful to hear his voice falling to a discreet whisper when, interviewing and collecting material for the biography, he comes to discuss this incident in the founder's life, and finds himself met with frowning faces and disapproving looks and gaunt fingers wagged in warning. It is not fanciful to suggest that he and the surviving friends of Columban must have been aware of the somewhat embarrassing episode. He keeps the silence better than Justinian did; which is a pity. It is from Columban himself, from his own words, that we obtain material to answer the question: why and how did the Irish monk allow himself to be drawn into the controversy?

Almost on his arrival at the frontiers of the Lombard kingdom, he was greeted by letters from a certain man. This man was Agrippinus, who has been identified as the bishop of Como. What he wrote disturbed Columban against Pope Boniface IV, a saintly man, as a person suspect of slipping into the sect of Nestorius.

Astounded, Columban refused to believe the charge, and replied briefly as best he could. The reply is not extant. Suspicion had been, however, implanted in his mind. Its growth was nurtured and fostered in the Lombard court, which was, in fact, a doubtful place to seek the truth about the Three Chapters. King Agilulf was an Arian, and Queen Theudelinda supported the schismatics. Colum-

ban's distress was intensified when he heard the pope re-
viled and called a partisan of heretics and a schismatic.
Holding to the principle that the Roman Church defends
no heretic against the Catholic faith—the negative nature
of the principle suggests that he was fighting in a corner—
he boasted and promised that the truth would emerge.

It would be very difficult to find a more fundamental
cause of grief and profound mental disturbance for the
Irish monk. It was earthquake and he was at the centre of
it. The charges against the pope struck most dangerously
at the whole fabric of a *pietas* which was held sacred by him
and the people of his island: the image of the pope as
successor of the man to whom Christ had said, *Tu es Petrus;*
the image of Rome as the place blessed and exalted by the
relics of Peter and Paul. Rome was great and famous as
the mother-city of a civilization, but it was not for that
glory that the Irish revered her. They had never heard the
tramp of the legions nor seen the Roman builders and
engineers at work on fortress and wall, road and bridge,
nor heeded Roman laws and government. Rome had sent
them the Faith. They were bound to St. Peter's chair, and
in their minds it was only on that chair that Roman fame
and greatness depended. The rest was dust. Rome was the
head of all the churches of the world. It was as simple as
that: *Roma orbis terrarum caput est ecclesiarum.* The
Latin, Columban's, is like a roll of drums beaten in the
pride of fidelity and in the pride of the people who, in the
island far off in the western ocean, had held the Faith un-
broken and never bred heretic, judaizer or schismatic.
Was this chair of Peter now really infamous?

He had another cause for personal action and it sprang from the missionary habit of his mind.

King Agilulf was distressed by the schism of his own subjects for the sake of the Catholic queen and of his son who was being reared a Catholic, and also for his own sake. He was reputed to have said that if he could discover for certain the truth of the controversy, he himself would believe. He requested Columban to write to the pope. This request amazed Columban, filled him with manifold solicitude, and even led him to believe that the miraculous was at work. For the Lombards had long trampled on the Catholic faith and affirmed the Arian heresy. But here was the Lombard king asking that the pope should make all men one flock of Christ as soon as might be, and bring peace quickly to the Faith and the country.

The letter that Columban wrote to Pope Boniface ran to some five thousand words, that is, it would require about forty minutes to be read aloud at an intelligible pace. We may be sure that he did read it aloud, probably to Queen Theudelinda if not to the king. For all his protestations of lowliness, rusticity, dullness and lack of ability in face of the successor of St. Peter, he writes with the verve and the gusto of a man who likes controversy and loves words with the passion of a poet. There are passages in which the clarity of sense grows dim under the colours of magnificent verbiage. He uses a vocabulary as rich and varied as an oriental bazaar. He draws on all the devices of alliteration and assonance that he knows; extends metaphors of the ship, the Church, sailing dangerously on a stormy ocean, and of an army being mustered for battle with the trumpets sounding together; introduces proverbs and the lan-

guage of domestic occupations; and, of course, puns. He inevitably puns on his own name in Hebrew, Greek and
Latin. And on the name of Vigilius! How could the connec-
tion of such a name with "vigil" escape? Repeatedly he
puns on the name. "Keep vigil, since perhaps Vigilius did
not keep vigil very well." *Vigila itaque, quaeso, papa, vigila, et iterum dico, vigila; quia forte non bene vigilavit
Vigilius.* . . .

What Columban said at great length could have been
said in far fewer words. Apart from being less tedious and
more effective in the argument, brevity might have forced
him to be more logical and lucid. But it would have lost us
this living evidence of the vigour and stormy pressure of his
personality. His manner, his nature, did not belong to the
cooler and more matter-of-fact style of Rome. Lacking any
reply from Pope Boniface, if indeed any reply was ever
sent, we can only wonder how the papal officials felt and
thought when they opened the parchment and began to
read the elaborate opening salutation:

"To the most beautiful Head of all the churches of the
whole of Europe, the most sweet Pope, the exalted ruler,
Shepherd of Shepherds, the most reverend Bishop, the
humblest to the highest, the least to the greatest, the rustic
to the city man, the inarticulate to the most eloquent, the
last to the first, the wanderer to the native, a poor little
creature to the most powerful,—and wonderful to relate, a
curious thing, a rare bird—the Dove dares to write to Pope
Boniface."

This series of elaborate verbal obeisances, like an oriental ritual approach to a potentate, are in direct and
startling contrast with the tone of most of the letter. In a

few minutes, the courteous murmur, the cooing of the
Dove, gives way to a voice raised so vehemently that the
commentators of later centuries, including the great Bos-
suet, have listened to it with awe and not a little shock.

"Who could listen to a baldpate?" Columban asks in yet
another obeisance. "Who would not say immediately: who
is this presumptuous babbler that dares to write without
being asked?"

The vehemence begins in the answer:

"To him I retort that there is no presumption when the
edification of the Church requires it; and if he takes exception to me personally, let him consider not who I am
who speaks but what I say. For how shall a wandering Christian keep silent about what your Arian neighbour has been
shouting for a long time? 'Better are the wounds of a friend
than the deceitful kisses of an enemy.' Others speak ill of
you in private; in sorrow and grief I shall dispute in public.
. . . For I grieve, I declare, for the disgrace of St. Peter's
chair. I know, however, that the affair is beyond me, and
that as the saying has it, I am thrusting my face in the fire
all at once. But what is face-saving to me before men when
it is necessary to show zeal for the Faith? . . . I shall speak as
a friend indeed, as a disciple, and as your follower, not as a
stranger; therefore I shall speak out freely, saying to our
masters and helmsmen of the spiritual ship and to the
mystic look-out men: Watch, for the sea is tempestuous
and in turmoil from the deadly squalls, because it is not
just one menacing wave which, even across a swelling
ocean, soars from the foaming whirlpools of a hollow rock
though it be from afar, and drives the sails before it, but it
is a full tempest of the element, surging and lashing on

every side, that threatens shipwreck of the mystic barque; and so I, a frightened sailor, dare to cry out: Watch, for the water has already entered the ship of the Church, and it is imperilled."

It is then, smelling the salt airs off the sea as it were, that he recalls how the Irish at the world's edge have ever been faithful Christians, and how he has tried to refute those men who revile the pope, and how he has replied to Agrippinus, who provoked his pen. From one traditional image he turns to another. He calls on the pope, the true shepherd, to come and stand between the sheep and the wolves, the many wolves of Italy whose cubs can now be scarcely exterminated.

"But may God wipe out such a breed, and pasture his flock and fight on your side; do you carry out your work as shepherd watchfully, standing on guard day and night, so that you may see the staff of almond-wood which afterwards you may be worthy to see in the shape of a hook in the time of gathering the true fruits. Therefore, that you may not lack apostolic honour, maintain the apostolic faith, confirm it by testimony, strengthen it by writing, defend it by holding a synod, that none may properly oppose you. Do not despise a foreigner's word of advice. . . . Do not fear to be held guilty of falsehood, for you have the truth which you ought to proclaim; many indeed, and this is a serious matter, are dejected in these parts of the land by the unconcern of the shepherds, and many are deceived by the prosperity of a most unhappy abundance. . . ."

Something of the prophet who professes to discern signs of the coming of doomsday now enters Columban's message. He warns the pope to rise from sleep because "in

the midst of perilous times we stand almost at the end."
Nations are troubled; kingdoms fall; soon the Most High
God will speak and the earth will be shaken. He, Columban, who is no brave soldier, sees how the armies of the
enemy have surrounded Christians. He importunes the
pope to rouse the sleeping leaders, form the battle-line
and enter in his own person into the vanguard because "for
a long time as has been apparent in this region, even we
Christians have been defeated in this spiritual war, first
by our carnal vices and worldly living, next by the in-
sipidity of wavering faith. . . . For the cause of all evils
is the blind security of prosperity."

He is surprised by the sloth which has overwhelmed
Christians. He begs the pope to act, to cut the lengthy
cord of error with St. Peter's knife, that is, with "a true
profession of faith in council and with an abhorrence and
anathematization of all heretics, so that the chair of Peter
may be purified of all error if any has been introduced,
and if not, so that its purity may be demonstrated to all
men. . . . But while I say this, not ignoring that in a
noisy, shrill and tumultuous mob there are many reasons
which do not permit a full investigation of these matters,
it is not because I give credit to them that I have spoken,
but because certain things ought to be done. If there are
any rebels against the truth among your fellow provincials,
let your condemnation include these alone; for a mouth
filled with flour or other stuff cannot blow up a fire. . . . So
call a council that you may be cleared of the charges laid
against you. . . . For you are reputed to favour heretics, as
I hear—far be it from us that this has been, is, or shall be
true. They say that Eutyches, Nestorius, and Dioscorus,

ancient heretics as we know, were accepted by Vigilius at
some council, the fifth I think. Here, they assert, is the
whole cause of the scandal; if, as they say, you also accept
thus, or if you know that Vigilius himself died under such
a taint, why do you recite his name against your conscience?"

When Columban refers to the recitation of the name of
the dead Pope Vigilius, he had in mind the ancient custom of the diptych. Diptychs were two-leaved, hinged
tablets of wood, ivory or metal on which names were inscribed on a film of wax. "Diptychs of the living" contained the names of the living pope, the bishops, princes
and benefactors of the Church, while the "diptychs of the
dead" contained the names of persons eminent for holiness
or Christian deeds. These names were read aloud during
the early centuries from the pulpit or the altar during the
Canon of the Mass, in which, in our time, vestiges of the
ancient usage may still be found. Exclusion from these
lists was a grave ecclesiastical penalty. What Columban
meant, then, was that the name of Vigilius should be ex-
cluded from the diptych of the dead if it was true that he
had been guilty of favouring heretics. But weak and
vacillating though Vigilius may have been, he was never
guilty of favouring such a conjunction of heretics as
Nestorius, who attributed two personalities to Our Lord,
Eutyches, who reacted against this teaching and suppressed
the human nature of Christ to save the divine, and Dioscoros, his ruffianly ally. It is quite evident that Columban
has been given an erroneous history of the affair of the
Three Chapters, a sort of folklore version that has filtered
down through the centuries to leave no more than a

muddle of names. All that complaisant imperial blundering begun before he was born, all that attempted violence
to truth and conscience, the conspiracies, forgeries, edicts
and chaffering arguments of inflamed monks, and the
whole dreadful earthquake of schism, becomes trans-
mogrified into a muddled accusation against Pope Boniface
IV.

Yet, it has not been noted sufficiently how Columban,
for all his vehemence, guards his assumptions with "if."
He does not say that things are thus and thus. He says
repeatedly, "if they are thus. . . ."

"You are already to be blamed if you have deviated
from the true Faith and 'made your first faith void'; justly
do your subordinates oppose you, and justly do they
hold no communion with you, until the memory of the
lost souls is erased and consigned to oblivion. For if these
things are certain rather than fictitious, your sons are
transposed topsy-turvily into the *head,* while you become
the *tail,* who have always held to the orthodox Faith, whoever these may have been, even if they appear to be your
subordinates; they themselves, however, are the orthodox
and true Catholics, who never favoured nor defended any
heretics or suspect persons, but zealously maintained the
true Faith."

It is rough speech to address to a pope. Columban is
conscious of it. Asking for forgiveness if his rough words
cause offence to pious ears, he explains that he speaks as
he does because the essential burden of history demands
total statement, because the liberty customarily allowed
in his own country makes him audacious, and lastly, because thinking on the membership of Christ's Body, he is

concerned for harmony and peace. Again, his mind goes back to Ireland, to the people bound to St. Peter's chair. They honour Rome less for her secular glory than for being the place which holds the relics of Peter and Paul, "those two fiery horses of God's Spirit" who drew the chariot of which Christ is the charioteer across the seas, across the swelling flood where the dolphins turn, "even to the Western regions of earth's farther stand." From that time, the papacy is great and famous, and Rome is herself nobler and more famed, and "Rome is the head of the churches of the world."

"And thus," he continues, "since your honour is great according to the dignity of your see, so you need to take great care lest you lose your dignity by some foolishness. For power will be in your hands so long as your principles remain sound; for he is the indisputed key-holder of the Kingdom of Heaven who by true knowledge opens to the worthy and shuts to the unworthy; otherwise, if he does the opposite, he will be unable either to open or shut."

He importunes the pope, successor of St. Peter on whom Our Lord bestowed the keys of the kingdom, to put an end to strife. It is the craft of Satan to divide the Body of Christ, to separate His members and part the vesture, which means the unity of the very Son of God. He pleads for an agreement, for a meeting, and for a refusal to argue about ancient matters of dispute. Certain things are clear. On these men he can come to a decision. Let it be made. Against Nestorius he states his credo, his belief in one Christ, "Who in His divinity is co-eternal with the Father and in His humanity is younger than His mother,

Who born in the flesh never departed from heaven, Who remaining in the Trinity, lived in the world."

"I beseech you for the sake of Christ, do not spare those who have tried to separate you from Christ."

He is now approaching the end of the immensely long letter that must have left a cramp in his aged fingers as he toiled over it. Consciousness of his station and of the manner of his speech never leaves him. He asks for pardon for hitting so hard and hurtfully. But on such a matter he cannot speak otherwise. He has tried in all things to conform to the truth and he has served God only.

"But when the Gentile Lombard king requests a doltish Irish pilgrim to write, when the current of the ancient flood returns, who will not wonder rather than cavil? Yet in God's cause I shall not tremble nor dread the tongues of men who lie more often than they utter truth, while, when needs demand it, we must resist diffidence rather than submit to cowardice. Therefore I beseech you, since many doubt the purity of your faith, that you will quickly remove this blotch from the good name of the Holy See, because this reputation of constant caprice does not accord with the seriousness of the Roman Church . . . For I believe that there is always a steadfast pillar of the Church in Rome. . . ."

In a most moving passage, of which the cadence is a prayer, he moves to the conclusion. He repeats how King Agilulf has asked him to write and so filled him with amazement and solicitude, but in hope, he remembers Christ the King.

"Perhaps Christ, by whose favour all good is born, now regards us affectionately. We are pitiful creatures indeed if

by our side the scandal is made greater. Thus, the King
begs, the Queen begs, and all beg that you, as quickly as it
can be done, should make all one, that as peace comes to
the country, peace should come to the Faith, that all from
first to last may be made one flock of Christ. Let the King
follow the King; and let you follow Peter; let the whole
Church follow you. What is more pleasant than peace after
war? What sweeter than the reunion of brothers after separation? How cheerfully does a father return after many
years? So, peace among His sons shall be joy to God
the Father for ever and ever, and the gladness of Mother
Church shall be an everlasting festival. As for the rest,
Holy Father and brethren, pray for me, a most miserable
sinner, and for my fellow pilgrims, beside the holy places
and the ashes of the saints, especially beside Peter and
Paul, men equally great as captains of the great King and
most valiant fighters on the field of victory, following the
Crucified Lord in death, that we may deserve to abide
in Christ, to please Him, to thank Him and praise Him
with the Father and the Holy Spirit, in your company
and with the saints, here and eternally for ever and ever.
Amen."

So the longest letter comes to an end with an affirmation
of Christian communion. If the reason for writing the
letter was a mistake, then it was a mistake that produced
one of the most magnificent acts of homage of those disturbed centuries to the chair of Peter. The essence of the
homage is briefly and forcefully contained in the lapidary
sentence that might be carved over the doorway of any
papal palace: *Tu Petrum, te tota sequatur ecclesia:* Let
you follow Peter, and let the whole Church follow you.

In six words, it gives the sense and intention of the five
thousand words over which the fiery old monk had
laboured in Milan.

With poor information, he had tried to play his part
honourably. Had he lived longer, he would have found
better information, but had he lived another fifteen years,
he might have been pained to the heart by the behaviour
or that rebellious monk of Luxeuil, Agrestius the trouble-
maker, whose abbot, Columban's successor, failed to restrain or hold him. Agrestius went to Aquileia and fell in
with the schismatics. As Jonas says, he cut himself off
from the whole Catholic world and condemned all who
remained united with the see of Rome. To Attala, Columban's successor in Bobbio, the last monastery to be founded,
he sent a venomous and insulting letter. Abbot Attala read
it, thought little of it, and gave it to Jonas to keep; and
Jonas kept it for a number of years but lost it through
carelessness.

CHAPTER 8

The Last Sojourn

1

WHILE Columban was still in Milan, a man called Jocundus came to King Agilulf and told him that he knew of a place in the Apennines where there was a church dedicated to St. Peter, fertile, well-watered land and good fishing in the rivers: in a word, a suitable site for a monastery. The name of the place was Bobbio.

It lay in high hilly country at the base of a mountain and at the confluence of the river Trebbia and the smaller stream, Bobbio, two waters that could be yellow roaring floods in winter and dry, rocky, gravelly ravines in the drought of summer. Jonas would tell about the floods and the winter cold in this high country. It was the sort of terrain in which the old abbot seemed to flourish—hilly, wild, watered, wooded and remote from cities. There was something to rebuild: the church of St. Peter was in ruins.

With whatever monks or novices had joined them in Milan, Columban set off on this seventy-mile journey, his last, across the Lombard plain and up the winding but not

difficult road to the Bobbio that would remember his name
during all the centuries when, in Bangor, it would be forgotten. He was probably happier and more serene than
he had been in the Lombard towns and palaces since he
left the Alps. He was moving away again from the affairs
of kings and townsmen, to find for the last time the detachment, the rural, nest-like enclosure in which he had
lived and developed, boy and man, in far-off Ireland and
in Gaul of the Merovingian kings.

By this time he must have known about the end of the
wars between the brothers and the terrible, obscene death
of Queen Brunhilde. The victorious Theuderich of Burgundy had died of dysentery in Metz five or six months
after the murder of the defeated Theudebert. For the
third time, Brunhilde was left alone with a child, her
great-grandson, to take care of. He was Sigisbert, Theuderich's eldest son. She called an assembly of the Franks
and ordered them to do homage to the boy as the ruler of
Burgundy and Austrasia, and for a while they accepted
him. But the Austrasians, hating the queen, conspired with
King Clothair of Neustria and joined his army when it
marched. Brunhilde fled to Burgundy and—incredible
woman—she raised an army, faced the Neustrians on the
headwaters of the Aisne, and was suddenly left unpro-
tected when all the fighting men joined the invader. All
Gaul was coming together as one, but it would cost her
everything. She fled with the boy king. They were pursued,
captured, and brought before King Clothair, who showed
the ancient brutal lust of his forebears. On his orders, the
old woman was flogged, stripped naked and displayed on
a camel's back for three days among the soldiers; and

then she was tied by the hair, hands and feet to wild horses which were lashed till they galloped among rocks and stones and battered and tore her body to pieces. Venantius Fortunatus had praised her beauty, but so she died. Columban, if some scholars are to be believed in the attribution, wrote a neat quatrain about her, with a reference in the last line to Our Lady:

> The wise mind flees the venomed tongue
> Of evil woman wagged in pride.
> Woman wrecked life's gathered crown;
> But woman gave long joys to life.

Jonas noted the end of that Merovingian tale as the fulfillment of Columban's three prophecies. The lines of Jonas's own destiny were being laid down by the southward march of the abbot through Lodi and Piacenza to meet the Trebbia river. It was the march of a man trying to disappear out of the world and out of history, but history as written by Jonas and made by kings and the people of Lombardy on the plains and in the mountains would not let Columban go. Yet, he almost disappears, to be heard about a little, and to die. The strangest and the last silence of Jonas is about the end of the founder. In the sort of hagiography he and his contemporaries wrote, descriptions of edifying deathbeds were at least as important as the prophecies and signs that preceded the births. Were Columban's last days so full of wonders, and therefore so well known, that Jonas did not bother to write about them?

2

The last days began with that southward march from the capital of the Lombard kingdom. An old tradition, coloured considerably by legend, can tell us something of the journey. If the tradition is correct topographically, Columban and his companions must have travelled along the shallow valley of the Lambro towards where it enters the serpentine course of the Po. In the level country between the two rivers, and set back from the road between Pavia and Piacenza, there rises a long low hill. It is gently sloped, wooded, and planted with vines, fig and cherry trees. From its height of a few hundred feet, it overlooks the lush irrigated and monotonous plain. On the northern lower slopes there was a community of peasants. The tradition has it that Columban stayed here among these people, to preach to them and to leave them such an image of himself as could endure for centuries. Most improbably, the tradition claims that he taught them the cultivation of the vine. Centuries later, at any rate, the name of the community became San Colombano. In the late ninth century, the property was recorded in a charter from King Berengarius as belonging to the monastery of Bobbio. In the parish church, two silver reliquaries are cherished. One, shaped like a forearm and hand, holds a finger of the saint. The other, about two feet high, preserves dust from his tomb in Bobbio; and around the sides are images of scenes from his life, such as the legendary planting of the vines and the acceptance of the deeds of the Bobbio monastic land from King Agilulf.

There is probably more subjective than objective truth in the tradition. It is only one manifestation of how astonishingly the work of those last years and the spiritual influence of the last monastery irradiated an enormous countryside with the energy of the abbot's personality. Bobbio was the centre. It provided the seclusion that he had always desired. All around him in this place where he was to die, the mountains, hills and the deep bed of the Trebbia formed his enclosure. The mountains were densely wooded with fir trees, oaks, chestnuts and beeches, and the hillsides were cultivated for olives, vines, figs and almonds. The benevolent king of the Lombards had been generous. The air was brisker than on the hot and humid plain. Indeed, it was more like the northern air he had first breathed in the island from which he had exiled himself. By the deeded gift of the king who asked for the prayers of the monks in return, Columban now possessed the land around the old ruined church of St. Peter within a perimeter of four miles.

Again, the resurrection from ruins began. Probably in the late spring or early summer, he and the monks, with whatever help they could find, repaired the ruined church with timbers cut far up on the mountainside. Jonas tells about the work, and for the last time, as Columban's biographer, he is filled with wonder. When the trees toppled among the rocks and declivities that were inaccessible to wagons, Columban and two or three others lifted the trimmed enormous trunks and carried them down the rough slopes, though thirty or forty men could not move them on level ground. This, Jonas says, was regarded by the abbot as a sign from heaven, and he exhorted his monks to continue the work with joy in their hearts.

Although we are not told that it happened, we must assume that monks came to help from some of the other foundations, and that peasants from the valleys also gave a hand in the new monastery. There was need of haste before the winter. Monastic accommodation had to be built, cells, a refectory, workshops and other offices; ground had to be broken for tillage; and the Bobbio stream had to be dammed to provide a race for the mill in which wheat grown on the monastery lands could be ground. And all this was achieved and directed by men who adhered to the meagre dietary, interrupted the long days regularly for prayers and the Divine Office, and endured their first harsh Apennine winter that could freeze the torrents in the gorges and fill the valley with the breathless silence of the snows.

Columban may well have wished for the everlasting silence that could isolate him from the world. The world remembered him. Far away in Gaul, King Clothair in his days of victory with all his enemies dead, recalled Columban's prophecies. In that mood which was probably compounded of genuine piety and superstitious fear, he sent to the monastery of Luxeuil for Eustasius, who was the abbot. He requested Eustasius to travel after Columban and to plead with him to return to the Vosges. Moreover, he offered to pay the expenses of the journey and to provide Eustasius with an escort of noblemen as an earnest of his good intentions.

Abbot Eustasius travelled to Bobbio to meet the founder, to whose robe he had clung on the day of banishment from Luxeuil. It was his last opportunity to see him. He stayed for some time with the glad old man. A whole world had

come and gone since they had met in Metz: battles, kings
fallen, monks departed on missions, Gall settled in the
Alps, the troubles with the schismatics, and Clothair on
the Merovingian throne. If he had not heard before,
Columban could now hear more about the obscene and
bestial degradation of Queen Brunhilde, against whom
vindictive fury had not ceased to operate when she was a
soiled bloody carcase at the feet of the horses. Her body
had been denied Christian burial. It had been burned like
offal outside the camp where the soldiers made a spectacle
of her death. But people who admired her had secretly
gathered the burnt bones and ashes and buried them in
the monastery of St. Martin in Autun, which she had built
and endowed. Even Columban, who had let her feel the
terrifying and not always wise ferocity of his zeal for God's
things, must have known the goodness that was in her. It
was her misfortune to have fallen among the Merovingians.
Nine centuries after her death, alms were being distributed
daily in her memory while historians had not yet tried to
do her justice.

It had been in her wrath that she had been the means of
Columban's banishment from Luxeuil, to which he now
refused to return at King Clothair's invitation. His refusal
was tactful. Having exhorted Eustasius to be a good abbot
and to preserve the monks in the bonds of holy discipline,
he instructed him to tell the king diplomatically that he
felt he could not return and to ask for royal assistance for
the monastery of Luxeuil. Typically, he also wrote a
letter of castigation to the king. It has not survived. That
such a letter was written at all shows that the peace of the
Apennines had not softened the zeal of the abbot.

Ten years earlier, he might have returned from a banishment at the invitation of a king offering such tokens of
good faith. But, as he quoted in a fine piece of verse about
time, change and old age:

Fleeting time gives, takes and lessens all things.
Spring, summer, autumn, winter, year by year return;
All things return, but not his age to man.

He was now approaching his seventy-fifth year, building
the last nest in the mountains, and once more seeking out
lonely caves where he could remain in solitary prayer in
the manner he had learnt in Ireland. The solitude and the
dimness of the cave take and enclose him. Except for a
few final lines, he disappears from the pages of Jonas when
he is already appearing as a force in the spiritual history
of northern Italy and in popular legends. Of this he knew
nothing. He was Columban the sinner to the last, serving
God as best he could, and preparing for death with prayer,
fasting, and prostrations on the cold mountain stone.
Indeed, as he withdrew from the new raw settlement still
littered with timber for building and wood-shavings,
masonry and stone chippings, and toiled up northeastwards
from Bobbio to one of the caves that opens on the face of
an overhanging cliff high above the Trebbia, he cannot
have considered that his life had been a success in worldly
terms; that is, if assessment in worldly terms was ever
indulged in by this man, whose self-sacrifice had been
always without calculation.

It is likely that nothing could have surprised him more
than the way in which his foundations in the Vosges and

the Apennines exploded, as it were, in waves of light over Gaul and Italy. His mother's strange dream of a sun shining from her bosom before his birth and filling the world with light was strangely fulfilled. Clothair and later kings in Gaul cherished, protected and endowed Luxeuil, and not only Luxeuil but the nearly five score and more monasteries for men and women that observed Columban's Rule in the seventh century, housed and nurtured saints, and gave great and saintly bishops to at least a dozen sees. Monks or pupils of Luxeuil founded monasteries at Cusance, Moutiers-Grandval, Besançon, Jussamoutier, Meaux, Altivillers, Jumièges, Novimoutier, St. Valéry, St. Quentin, Jouet, Charenton, and Nevers. Disciples and monks of Columban were bishops of Rouen, Thérouanne, Vermandois, Noyon, Laon, Meaux, and Verdun. All this came about within half a century after his death, and less than three quarters of a century since his arrival in Gaul with twelve men from Ireland.

In that time, the monastic as well as the secular world was changing. That son of Duke Waldelenus and Flavia, Donat, who became bishop of Besançon and founded a monastery there, introduced items from the Rule of St. Benedict into Columban's, as did later abbots of Luxeuil itself. The forms of the Irish and Italian minds were mingling, and Monte Cassino and Bangor were being inscribed on the same spiritual map. Monastic and human necessity brought about the conjunction.

It is unrealistic to say that under Columban himself, there had been no provision for the election of abbots and office holders, for the relations between abbot and community, monks and novices, and for domestic routine.

Without being set down on parchment, that domestic
routine and system of domestic government were part of
the tradition the Irish monks had brought with them,
drilled into their very natures by discipline and long
practice, instinctive in them like the reactions of veteran
soldiers.

The rapid manner in which Annegray, Luxeuil, and
Fontaines were set up in working order, not to speak
of Bobbio, which was established by an old man, was
evidence of a tradition of operation that included the details of routine and discipline. But when Columban and
his pioneers died or departed, something written did become necessary. Moreover, what he had already written
made demands that were enormous. They were conditions
for heroes, utterly ascetic, obedient, self-sacrificing, and
disdaining even the smallest comfort of the body. One does
not minimize the glory of the Benedictine Rule by saying
that in comparison as well as in reality it made life in the
Columbanian monasteries look more like a frontline under
perpetual fire in an unceasing battle. Gradually, this Rule
supplanted Columban's, until Columban himself was described in an inscription in Bobbio as a disciple and follower of St. Benedict. In the old matter of the date of
Easter, the monasteries conformed. Though many of them
obtained and jealously preserved immunity from episcopal jurisdiction, the exotic isolation began to dissolve,
and while, of course, the *clausura* was defended and up-
held, the communities took on the colours and the accents
of the people and culture in which they were established.

Such change was inevitable. In Bobbio, the process was
perhaps quickest of all, because, as far as we know, there

was only one man in the monastery who was Irish by
birth and training, and he was Columban himself. The
next three abbots, whom Jonas knew and served, were men
of Luxeuil who had been reared in Gaul. Attala, the son of
a Burgundian noble, had been with Columban in Luxeuil.
Bertulf, son of the noble but pagan family, had lived under
the guidance of Abbot Eustasius and was taken by Attala
to Bobbio where, in 625, he became the next and third
abbot by the unanimous vote of the monks. It was in his
company that Jonas travelled to Rome to obtain from
Pope Honorius exemption from episcopal jurisdiction.
Bobolenus, the fourth abbot, was the son of an old friend
of Columban's, the amiable, inquisitive Winioc, who was
probably a Breton. There were then one hundred and fifty
monks in the monastery. It was to Bobolenus, and to
Waldebert, third abbot of Luxeuil, that Jonas dedicated
his book about the founder. During his term of office,
Abbot Bobolenus wished to establish even more firmly
and to extend the exemption accorded by Pope Honorius.
With the help of the Lombard rulers, he obtained con-
firmation of the privilege in 643 from the Greek Pope
Theodore I and, as well, other privileges which allowed
bishops to visit the monastery only by the invitation of
the abbots, who were made directly responsible to the
Holy See. By that time the monastery was most prosperous,
and its monks were preaching to the Arian and half-pagan
peoples of Lombardy and diffusing the cult of the founder.
Their monastery would adopt the Benedictine Rule and
share for nearly a thousand years in the fortunes of the
great Order. The Bobbio library would grow with the
donation and acquisition of manuscripts and books of

Christian and pagan authors which included Columban's own commentary on the Gospels (lost like so much else of his), works by St. Augustine, St. Cyprian, St. Isidore, Cassian, Bible texts, Pope Gregory's *Dialogues,* Virgil, Ovid, Terence, Juvenal, Lucretius, Cicero, Martial and Seneca. Scholars of the Renaissance would forage greedily in the library; abbots would give books away; high churchmen would take them, until at last, all would be scattered among some of the famous libraries of Europe, the Ambrosian in Milan which holds the Antiphonary of Bangor, the Vatican, Turin, Naples and Vienna. But like the books that were scattered, many bearing the superscription *Liber S. Colombani di Bobbio,* something of Columban was propagated across the land of Italy.

His cult was diffused from Piedmont to the Adriatic, and from Lake Como to the frontiers of Latium. By the eleventh century, an abbot of Bobbio, Gerbert the Frenchman who became Pope Sylvester II, could wonder at how much of Italy had become Columban's spiritual possession. Legends about Columban flowered in the northern Apennines, on the Ligurian coast and on the plains of Lombardy. Plants were called by his name as if they had sprung up in his footsteps or under his benediction. In Tuscany, a variety of grape bears his name. He became the gentle thaumaturge. To the cave northeast of Bobbio and above the Trebbia, mothers used to bring sick children that they might be healed by laying them down where the old Irish monk had knelt and prayed until he could pray no more.

3

The silence of the cave envelops him towards the end. He is no longer to be seen. The autumn of 615 moves through the thick fall of leaf and nut, the last of the vintage, the crushing of the olives, the gathering of the figs that have been drying in the sun, and the storing of the grain in the little mill on the Bobbio. The rivers are filling up for the days of the roaring floods that scour out the courses with grinding stones and gravel, bushes and trees and the debris of the mountains. There is need of glowing charcoal and log fires. In the darkness of the lengthening nights when the monks, led by the aged abbot, go to recite the Hours in the restored church of St. Peter, the air is bitter cold.

We can hardly see him at all at the beginning of this, his second and last winter in the Apennines. How have his years marked him, his thin handsome face, his great strength? He knew well about the bodily discomforts of old age, *tremebunda senectus:* the shrunken limbs with the loose laps of wrinkled skin, the stiffened knee joints, the nights when every sound meant a break in shallow sleep, and the blood freezing in every vein. Had he not noted the signs in the hexameters he wrote to someone named Sethus when he echoed the grave magisterial Latin voices he had loved so much, Horace, Virgil, Ovid and others?

By the reckoning of any hard-living men, old campaigners in the imperial wars or adventurous traders or pilgrims to distant holy places or even the serfs labouring

in the fields of ancient estates, he had given himself a hard
life, not just intermittently as a soldier who might retire
at the end of his service or as a traveller who could go
home at last, but continuously, ruthlessly and inexorably.
Before the impulse of his zeal, there had been no halt
for temporary easement and no expectation of rest from
battle or from the march along the pilgrim road except
in what lay at the other side of death. This side of death,
there was only flux, change, inconstancy. By his actions
and his words, all expressions of his integrity, he showed
a painfully intense awareness of the uncertainty of mortal
life—brief, fleeting, changeful, unstable, fickle, something
that even as it flowed and fled men must flee from and hold
themselves rather as lovers and merchants of God and of
eternal life. From this sprang his profound restlessness. It
was divine nomadism, dangerous in men who had neither
his self-discipline nor his fixity of purpose.

Viae enim finis nostrae patria nostra est. For the end of
our road is our home. To reach that home, everything
must be sacrificed. We must give away, he preached, whatever we love apart from Christ for Christ's sake, life itself
by martyrdom if it be necessary, and if we are not given
that blessedness, then life by mortification. "Thus let us
live to Him Who while He lives is life for us; and let us
die to ourselves that we may live to Christ; for we cannot
live to Him unless we first die to ourselves, that is, die to
our wills. Let us be Christ's, not our own. . . ." *Christi
simus, non nostri.* That man loves well who hates himself,
that is, disciplines himself savagely. Life is a time of war
in which no one should expect rest, because in warfare
no man sleeps. What he preached, he practised and ex-

pected others to practise, his monks according to the rule, and layfolk, kings and queens according to the gospel. Hence his energy, his ferocity, his impatience and his rough speech, and his odd reluctance to reveal sentiment. He could be gentle with the afflicted and the miserable, the poor and the criminals, and savage with the mighty. He could love the brethren with a tenderness to draw tears and treat them, even in their sickness, with harshness. But he did not forget them. One of them, Gall, he did not forget when during the last week of that November, 615, he knew he was about to die.

He had laid a most fearful penance on his native friend and companion and had received in return the obedience he had expected. As he lay near death he commanded that his staff, the *cambutta* which had gone with him along the roads of half of Europe, should be sent to Gall as a token of absolution. Then, in the early hours of that Sunday morning, he died.

Hundreds of miles away to the north, Gall and his monks had finished Matins and were returning to their beds in the monastery they had built in the upland beside the river Steinach. As dawn was breaking, Gall roused his deacon, Magnoald, and said to him:

"Make everything ready for the service of Mass so that I may celebrate the divine mysteries without delay."

Astonished, Magnoald asked: "Will you yourself celebrate Mass?"

And Gall explained: "After the vigils of this night just ended, I learnt in a vision that my lord and father, Columban, had passed from the miseries of this life to Paradise. Therefore, I must offer Mass for his repose."

The bell was sounded, the monks entered the oratory, and Mass was offered up for the dead Columban. After Mass, Gall said to Magnoald: "My son, do not think it too much if I ask this request of you. Set out immediately for Italy and travel till you reach the monastery of Bobbio. Inquire there carefully about all that has happened to my abbot, and if you find he is dead, note well the day and the hour, so that you may discover whether my vision be true. When you have found all, come back and tell me."

It was winter, the season of short daylight. The road was long. Magnoald was young. He knelt at Gall's feet and pleaded that he did not know the way. But Gall reassured him, telling him not to be afraid because God would direct his steps.

In obedience, Magnoald made the journey. When he reached the monastery of Bobbio, he found that everything had happened just as Gall had seen in the vision. He stayed one night. The monks gave him a letter recounting the last hours of Columban and, as well, the staff of forgiveness. Travelling hard, he returned to the north to give staff and letter to the abbot, Gall. And Gall wept.

Viae enim finis nostrae patria nostra est.

Jonas the Biographer

COLUMBAN'S first biographer was Jonas, the monk of Bobbio, who entered the monastery in 618. It may have been one of his private griefs that he missed a meeting with the founder by a handful of years, but in other ways he was fortunate.

He was a native of the little town of Susa, a hard six-day journey to the north in the Cottian Alps. In Susa itself, and in Bobbio, he received a fairly sound literary education. He read in Livy and Virgil, and in the classic lives of Christian saints, what St. Athanasius had written about Anthony, the founder of monasticism; St. Jerome's writings about those heroes of the eremetical life, Paul and Hilarion; the writings of Sulpicius Severus about St. Martin of Tours; St. Hilary's life by Fortunatus, and St. Ambrose's by Paulinus of Milan. His reading made him useful as a secretary to Abbot Attala, whom he revered as a living saint, and it also aroused in him the desire to set down the life of the founder.

The abbot, Attala, could tell him much at first hand, as could other monks he met in Bobbio and, later, during his travels in northern countries where the founder had worked. The temper of Jonas's mind was not, however, creative or very critical. He had many talents but no genius worth speaking of. He belonged to his environment and to his time, and he showed this particularly in his purpose as a biographer. He wished to instruct, to build in the minds and hearts of people the image of sanctity which the founder had become; that is, he wished to edify.

The next abbot of Bobbio, Bertulf, could also tell him a great deal that was useful for his purpose. Bertulf, a native of Gaul and son of a noble pagan family, had been a monk in Luxeuil, where he had lived a life of the most scrupulous adherence to the founder's Rule. In the summer of 628 Jonas was one of the company that set off with Abbot Bertulf for Rome to discuss with Pope Honorius certain problems that the founder had bequeathed, one concerning the tedious question of the observance of Easter. The pope was pleased with Father Bertulf and in the matter of jurisdiction the monastery was exempt, but the pope kept the monks so long in the increasing heat of Rome that Bertulf fell ill and nearly died on the road back to Bobbio.

2

Not long after the return to Bobbio from Rome, Jonas was off on his travels again, sent by Abbot Bertulf to visit the monastery of Luxeuil in Gaul. It is not unjust to him to say that he, like so many of the monks who accompanied and followed Father Columban, was becoming filled with the *desiderium peregrinandi,* that yearning to go on pilgrimages which without strict discipline and legitimate objectives could produce dangerously footloose monks. His stability was, apparently, beyond doubt. The immediate purpose of his journey, probably the most fruitful for him as a biographer in search of material, may well have been to inform Abbot Eustasius of Luxeuil about the success of the mission to Pope Honorius. But there was yet another abbot to whom the information must have been a cause of joy. A meeting with him must have seemed to Jonas like a meeting with the *alter ego* of Columban himself.

This abbot was Gall. Jonas must have already known the story of how Columban and Gall had parted on a tragic day on the shore of Lake Constance and of how years were to pass before there was full forgiveness. There was compact in that story such strong elements of charity, affection, authority, obedience, harshness and meekness, that Jonas may be pardoned if, as a biographer, he turned from the mystery in silence. But there were other things to learn from Gall and Jonas learned them. Not enough, perhaps, for a biographer with a broader and less didactic purpose. Of all the people Jonas met and would meet, Gall was nearest to the founder, not so much in character, for he was more tranquil, and temperate (like the good fisherman he was!), as in culture and training, and in native experience of the strange island God had left on the edge of the known world where the empires fortunately forgot it. Gall was the monk to whom the founder had bequeathed his staff. He was, in a sense, the founder's eldest son.

In Luxeuil, Jonas met Abbot Eustasius among others, and he was lucky to arrive in time because the abbot had not long to live. To have missed conversing with him would have meant a serious deficiency in the essential eye-witness accounts on which the biography of the founder was to be based. Eustasius had been Columban's *minister* or secretary, and he had almost worshipped him as a loving son might worship the best of fathers. After the founder's death he tried very faithfully to live according to that giant image. He preached to the heathen, restored the sick and the maimed, and ensured that his monks adhered to the stern Rule. During his time the number of monks increased so much that it was obvious other monasteries would need to be established in the neighbourhood to hold them. Some of his monks or disciples became abbots themselves, and many became bishops. But all this was not accomplished without misfortunes. Like Columban himself, like Attala and Bertulf, he met with adversities that saddened many years of his life. The story of those adversities should have given Jonas a deeper knowledge of men, and especially of men who ought not to be monks.

The cause of the unhappy days in Luxeuil was a young monk named Agrestius who wanted to go off preaching to pagan peoples before he was fit for the work. He was in-experienced, poor in self-discipline, overzealous and very headstrong. Reluctantly, Abbot Eustasius had to let him have his way. Agrestius preached without effect in northern Italy where, possibly through ignorance, he joined some persuasive schismatics whose existence had been of great moment in a long sad chapter in the founder's life. Agrestius condemned his former friends who remained in communion with Rome, and he sent an abusive letter to Abbot Attala of Bobbio, a letter which Jonas the secretary lost through carelessness. Next Agrestius returned to Luxeuil to try and win over Abbot Eustasius who, of course, was also lamentably in error! He was met with gentleness and argument, but at last he was driven out of the monastery. Thereupon, he directed his attacks against the very foundations of the spiritual life which Columban had left to his sons. This unfilial act stimulated Jonas to one of his rare outbursts of vituperation. He described Agrestius as a filthy hog grunting and hissing through his teeth. An attack on Columban was more than he could take with meekness. Through a bishop who was his cousin, Agrestius now tried to inveigle King Clothair of Gaul into making common cause with him against Luxeuil, but Clothair had been Columban's friend. (What a story Jonas had to tell about how that friendship came about in the fall of kingdoms!) At Clothair's request, the bishops met in synod at Mâcon in 626 and Agrestius was called upon to put forward his charges. This was his chance, but the firebrand must have disappointed both his allies and opponents. He accused Columban and Eustasius of having introduced novelties which were alien to the canons of the monastic life. On being questioned for specific instances, he declared that the monks according to the Rule frequently made the sign of the Cross over the spoons with which they supped, and that they asked blessings when entering or leaving any of the monastic buildings. It was all true, but it was only one part of the Irish custom of asking a blessing in the name of the Trinity on almost every act and gesture, on vessels, food, fields, doorways, gates and journeys. In such intense and proliferate devotions, the bishops in synod could find no cause for condemnation. Again, they asked Agrestius if he had any other grounds for complaint. Desperately, he said that Father Columban had added prayers to the collects of the Mass and many other superfluous things which, along with their author, should be execrated as heresy. Agrestius had gone too far.

He was easily answered. He was refuted in a noble speech by Abbot Eustasius, who said that it was perfectly lawful for the monks to use the sign of the Cross in their every action, and that the addition of prayers was something that occurred in every church. Then, as Agrestius continued to mumble other petty charges, he said:

"In the presence of these bishops, I, disciple and successor of him whose rule and foundation you condemn, invite you to appear within a year before the divine tribunal to make your charges, so that you may experience the just judgment of Him Whose servant you have tried to defile with your calumnies."

It was, as Jonas may have reflected, rather like the terrifying voice of Columban himself, who did not fear to summon kings, queens, and even popes, to just judgment. Something of Columban spoke through Eustasius. Something of Columban's own story was revealed in the manner in which Agrestius, after he had continued his intrigues and subversion, met a sudden and violent death under the axe of a slave with whose wife, it was rumoured, he had misconducted himself. How many of Father Columban's terrible prophecies had come to such bloody fulfillment! So in the company of Abbot Eustasius in Luxeuil Jonas was able to collect not only first-hand stories about the founder but also first-hand stories about the history of the foundations. If when he came to write he occasionally refrained through economy from describing events which might be assumed to be commonly known and in documentary form, or through tact from turning over the bones of controversies that were best left to the decency of silence, it was not because his functional method of biography made him manipulate the truth. For he was most truthful. He did not hesitate to recount curious stories either about the founder or some of the monks. The founder could seem harsh. So be it. Monks could be scandalous fools. So be it also.

3

The next time Jonas tells us about himself is about the year 639, and he is back in the monastery at Bobbio. He is no longer a young novice listening in awe to stories about Father Columban. He has travelled much, busied himself with inter-monastic affairs, conversed with a great variety of people, and prodigiously increased his knowledge of Columbanian foundations. He has met and talked for days with men who laboured with the Irishman; he has lived in the monastery of Luxeuil, and at least seen the neighbouring foundations, Fontaines and, the first of all, Annegray. He has walked fields that were wild mountain land before the monks felled trees and cleared brushwood and dug stubborn roots from the earth. Who was better fitted to write Columban's life? He has read much and his pen is practised. His abbot in Bobbio, shrewd Bertulf, and the brethren, all urge him to write. In fact, Abbot Bertulf expresses his wish that Columban's life should be written by Jonas, and the abbot's wish is a command.

If Jonas is ready, destiny is not. Before he can sit down with quills and parchment among the books and papers in the monastery he is called or sent away for three years on a long and laborious journey to the far north. Like Father Columban he now experiences in his own flesh and spirit the hardships, the process of exile, and the isolation, joys and many heartbreaks of the Christian missionary preaching among pagan peoples.

He was called, how we do not know, to the northern country around the banks of the Scarpa, the Elnon and the Schelde, and along the seacoast. It was cold country enough and quite monotonous for a man who had lived in the Alps and the Apennines and enjoyed the Italian abundance of the fruit, grain and wine that had attracted invaders like the Lombards. The physical comforts of the broken civilization of home, even the austere physical comforts of a monastery, were unknown in the flat lands, the marshes, the dunes and the forests. Jonas never grumbled; at least, not in his writings. He worked under the direction of Amand, the saintly bishop with no fixed see who, after years of prayer as a hermit in Bourges, had settled in these parts to preach the gospel. Jonas tells us little about the bishop or, for that matter, about himself, except that he travelled a great deal, sometimes by ash-canoe. The mission lasted a few years. Then, Jonas is journeying again.

We next find him in Gaul, where he discovers yet more evidence of the creative spirit of the founder, which was in fact more active after his death, as if he had been a great oak that, before it fell, scattered acorns to produce a wood. At Meaux on the river Marne, Father Columban had once been welcomed in days of grievous misfortune by one of the noble Christian households of Merovingian Gaul. His visit had been like an angel's come to set a seal of dedication on the children of the house. One son became a monk in Luxeuil and later bishop of Laon. He was one of Jonas's eyewitnesses. Another became a long-reigning bishop of Meaux and a founder of monasteries under the Rule brought by the Irishman. And not far from Meaux between the waters of the Grand-Morin and the Aubetin, their sister who had been a little child when she was dedicated by Father Columban founded at the age of twenty one of the greatest of the convents for women at Evoriacum, now called Faremoutiers. Century after century it was to grow and become famous as a school for the daughters of nobles and kings; and kings of France would endow it munificently. It was yet young and the foundress, Burgundafora, was still alive— another eye-witness—when wandering Jonas visited it and said the Month's Mind Mass there for the soul of one of the most blessed of the dead nuns, Sister Gibitrud, whose cell where her body lay was filled with the odour of balsam. Jonas himself would remember and record how as he said Mass the church was pervaded by a fragrance as of precious ointments and perfumes all blended together. It was probably here at Evoriacum he sat down at last, sometime before the year 643, took his notes from his satchel and began to write what he had been destined to write so that men might not forget what manner of man Columban of Ireland had been.

There were new abbots in Luxeuil and Bobbio. To

them he addressed the work that had been so long in the making:

"To the Fathers Waldebert and Bobolenus, most distinguished masters, highly honoured in holy rule, strong in the virtues of religion—Jonas, a sinner:

"I recall that some three years ago while I was staying in Bobbio during my wandering in the country of the Apennines, I promised at the entreaties of the brethren and at the command of Abbot Bertulf to write an account of the life and work of our beloved Father Columban, especially as very many of those who had lived with him and had seen his work were still alive. . . ."

He confesses that despite love of the brethren and respect for the wishes of Abbot Bertulf, he has long refrained from starting on the work because he thought himself inadequate. Now, the work was done. He asks that any lack of eloquence in it should be supplied; he asks for correction for the sake of his readers so that they may not be repelled from imitating the virtues of the saints through any clumsiness of expression or through want of conformity with the truth. If he praises any person who is still alive, he hopes he will not be accounted a flatterer but rather a recorder of a deed well done.

He works hard to make his preface stylish, though at least one commentator has remarked on his barbarous Latinity.

He submits his writings to be weighed in the balance by the fathers, so that when they have given their approval, others may not doubt. But if any reader finds something not duly clear or distinct, let him reject it, particularly if he is possessed of the eloquence and learning of the scholars. Such a reader must know, however, that he, Jonas, does not aim at being counted among them. And then in a series of ironical antitheses, he apologizes for what he has done, poor stuff compared with what the scholars could do:

"They, drenched with the dews of eloquence, have adorned the green fields with flowers; for us the arid earth will hardly produce a shrubbery. They are rich in the gum of the balsam tree of Engaddi and the perfumes of Arabia; we must be content with butter from Ireland. They draw peppers and spice from India; for us, the dim pine-bearing ranges of the Apennines, numbed by the cold west winds, will scarcely grow even the saliunca. They glory in the variety of precious stones; we in the amber of Gaul. They seek the exceedingly exotic fruits of the palm tree; for us, as the poet of Italy has put it, the mild fruit of the tender chestnut."

It was on an eclogue of Virgil's he drew in those last words for fine feathers to give his style wings. The Apennine land was good. That he knew. He was proud of his native Susa above which the chestnut woods crowded to meet the descending march of the pines. Chestnuts and pinenuts were good; and hungry monks in times of abundance and of famine could be glad to eat them roasted or crushed to a porridge or boiled with honey according to some receipt of the people who thanked God for them. But there was butter from Ireland: *nobis ex Hibernia vix butyrum pinguescit!* Had he tasted some of it that had come in a firkin on a wine-ship returning from a southern or eastern harbour on the Irish coast to one of the northern ports of Gaul? Was it really a symbol, full for him of a

domestic poetry, nourishing, wholesome, salty, and capable
of arousing some sort of vision of quiet pastoral life in
patriarchal farmsteads, of flocks and herds drifting as they
grazed across deep fields of grass between the dripping
Irish woods; while overhead the clouds came billowing in
vast processions from the Atlantic—the very fearful edge
of the world itself? In a prefatory poem he wrote, his mind
went out to the sea beating up in spume and foam around
that distant coast.

Acknowledgement

Before listing some of the books consulted, I should like to record my gratitude for the help given me by Father John Ryan, S. J., Father Smith and Father O'Neill of the Columban Fathers, Mr. Dominic O'Riordan, Mr. Vincent Grogan, and by my wife, who typed the book from my difficult manuscript.

Concannon, Helena, *The Life of Saint Columban* (Dublin, 1915)

Daniel-Rops, Henri, *The Miracle of Ireland* (Dublin, 1959)

Dawson, Christopher, *The Making of Europe* (London, 1934)

Dillon, Myles, *Early Irish Society* (Dublin, 1954)

Dubois, Marguerite-Marie, *Saint Columban* (Paris, 1950)

Gougaud, L., *Les Chrétientés celtiques* (1911)

Joynt, Maud, *The Life of St. Gall* (London, 1927)

Kendigren, Perry F., *The Poems of St. Columbanus* (1951)

Krusch, Bruno, *Ionae Vitae Sanctorum Columbani Vedastis, Iohannis* (1905)

McCarthy, E. J., S.S.C., *Saint Columban* (Nebraska, 1927)

MacNeill, Eoin, *Celtic Ireland* (Dublin, 1921)

——*Early Irish Laws and Institutions* (Dublin, 1936)

Mélanges Colombaniens: Actes du Congrès International de Luxeuil, 20-23 juillet 1950 (Paris, 1950)

Metlake, George, *The Life and Writings of St. Columban* (1914)

Moss, H.St., L.B., *The Birth of the Middle Ages* (Oxford, 1935)

Murphy, Gerard, *Early Irish Lyrics* (Oxford, 1956)

Pochin-Mould, Daphne, *The Celtic Saints* (Dublin-London, 1956)

Ryan, John, S.J., *Irish Monasticism* (Dublin, 1931)

CARMELITE MONASTERY
Beckley, Hill

Barrgkley

DATE